Cologne & Bonn, Germany

A Starting-Point Guide

Barry Sanders – writing as:

B G Preston

Cologne & Bonn, Germany

ISBN: 9798391698258

1st edition – June 2023-10Ar

Acknowledgements: The author greatly appreciates Sandra Sanders' contributions. She provided substantial editorial assistance to ensure the accuracy of this work.

Photography: Photos and maps in the Starting-Point Guides are a mixture of those by the author and other sources such as Adobe Media, Wikimedia, and Google maps. No photograph or map in this work should be used without checking with the author first.

~ ~ ~ ~ ~ ~

What we look for in a travel guidebook can vary by each individual. Some travelers want great details into the history of every monument or museum, others may want details on area restaurants. This guide's coverage has a bit broader approach. The goal of every Starting-Point Guide is to help orient you to the city and area, gain an understanding of its layout, how to get around, highlights of the town's treasures, and what is nearby.

Overviews are provided on the town, suggested lodging, points-of-interest, travel, and the area. Few details are provided on restaurants and shops or historical details on monuments.

The end goal is for you to come away from your visit having a good understanding of what is here, what the town is like, how to get around and not feel that you have missed out on leading sights and attractions.

Happy Travels, *B G Preston*

Contents

~ ~ ~ ~ ~ ~

A view of the iconic Cologne Cathedral and the Hohenzollern Bridge crossing the Rhine River.

Cologne, or Köln,[1] is Germany's fourth largest city and is well known for its magnificent cathedral, but there is much more to this city and area than this grand structure. When combined with its neighbor, Bonn (the two cities are considered to be one large

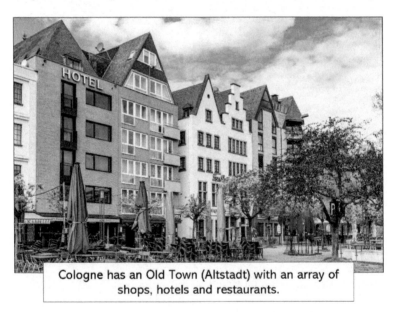

Cologne has an Old Town (Altstadt) with an array of shops, hotels and restaurants.

[1] **Cologne vs Köln vs Koeln. Kölsch**: Each of these words are appropriate for Cologne. Köln is the German version. The name of Cologne is used in this guide for naming simplicity, unless "Köln" is a formal name and identifier of a location or attraction.

metroplex), the array of attractions here is quite large. Put simply, this set of two cities on the Rhine is a great destination and they are the sole focus of this guide.

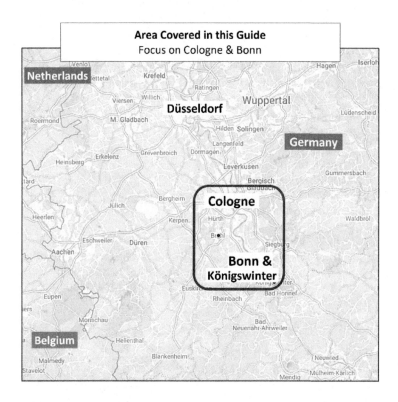

To help you have a successful visit to these towns in the Cologne-Bonn Region[2], several basic suggestions are outlined in this preface. After substantial travel by the author with some trips going better than others, the following guidelines have proven to help you have a great time.

---

[2] **Cologne Bonn Region:** This is a formal subset of the larger Ruhr Metropolitan Region which includes such cities as Düsseldorf.

Suggested Itinerary for a Multi-Day Trip:

If your travel schedule allows and you can visit here for more than a day trip, **plan on staying at least 2 nights in Cologne.** An option is to stay in Bonn, but there is no need to stay in both towns.

Traveling to Cologne for a quick trip from either Brussels or Frankfurt can be done if you only have one day available. See chapter 2 for guidance on traveling to this area. For a one-day trip, consider focusing only on central Cologne and perhaps visiting one or more of the attractions outlined in chapters 6 and 7.

COLOGNE

A two-night itinerary would, for example, allow you to: (a) arrive early or midday on your first day and become oriented to central Cologne and then explore some of the top attractions such as the cathedral and chocolate museum; (b) after your first night here, spend a half day taking fun tours such as a Rhine boat tour, riding the cable car over the river or perhaps pop down to Bonn; then (c) after your second night here, have a relaxing breakfast and head out to your next destination.

Consider an Area Discount Card:

When staying in an area filled with attractions, it can be valuable to purchase a local discount card. For Cologne, the **"Köln Card"** is offered and gives travelers discounts not only on attractions in the city, but discounts to many area tours, restaurants, and shops as well. If your preference is to stay in Bonn, that city has a discount card program as well, the Bonn Regional Welcome Card.

Acquire one if you are likely to visit multiple attractions, use local transportation, and take local tours. Do not acquire one if you will only visit one or two attractions during your stay. These passes can always be purchased in the Tourist Offices and are available online prior to your trip.

When visiting here, you will have the option of purchasing this card in increments of 24 or 48 hours. Individual and group pass options are available.

See chapter 4 for details on this program or visit the website at **www.Cologne-Tourism.com.**

Visit a Tourist Office:

For an initial visit to a city, unless you have a specific agenda, visiting the local tourist information office is often a good idea. Even if you have your plans in place and feel you know the city well, the personnel in these offices can provide substantial help.

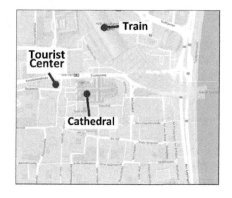

In Cologne, the Tourist Information Office sits directly across the plaza from the cathedral entrance and is also just a two-block walk to the train station.

They offer many city and area tours. This location is also where many tours start. Another plus in working with the personnel here is that they can sell the local city card and provide guidance on using the local transportation system which is included in the card.

- Cologne Tourist Office Address: Kardinal-Höffner Platz 1, 50667 Köln. **www.Cologne-Tourism.com**
- Bonn Tourist Office Address: Windeckstraße 1, 53111, Bonn. **www.Bonn.de**

~ ~ ~ ~ ~ ~

Understand the local Transportation Systems:

If you are likely to visit multiple attractions in or near Cologne, and are not driving, gaining an understanding of their excellent transportation system can be helpful. Using a local network of trams can also be fun and help you understand the layout and nature of the city.

In Cologne, the **Cologne-Stadtbahn** network (KVB) of trams services not only Cologne, but several neighboring towns as well. There are a dozen different lines with over 200 stations, so it is comprehensive. It is also a bit daunting to learn at first. This tram system is also a mixture of

Cologne has an extensive tram network.
Photo Source: Superbass-Wikimedia Commons

ground-level, above-ground, and subway lines which adds to the learning curve.

This is another area where the personnel in the Tourist Office can be very helpful. They will be able to help you acquire passes and explain how the system works.

Chapter 5 of this guide provides further information on Cologne's transportation network. Guidance on the transportation within Bonn may be found in chapter 12.

Download Some Apps: [3]

With the incredible array of apps for Apple and Android devices, almost every detail you will need for a great trip is available up to and including where to find public toilets. The apps range from those created by official agencies such as the Tourist Office and area train service to several which are put together by individual app developers. Following are a few recommended by the author.

The Cologne/Köln Guide by ETIPS is one of several apps which provide detailed and interactive guidance.

- **Cologne Travel Guide**: Provided by ETIPS, a firm which produces guide apps for numerous cities. Details attractions, transportation, hotels, and restaurants.

- **KVB App:** The Cologne public transportation system app. Detailed route planner for trams and buses and ability to buy passes via the app.

- **Map of Cologne:** Helpful and well detailed street maps for Cologne and suburbs.

- **Cologne Cathedral:** This popular destination is massive and having this app at hand when you view it will help you navigate through the complex and understand the history of the treasures around you.

---

[3] **Detailed Street Maps Note:** This guide does not include detailed street maps for the simple reason that no printed guidebook or map can be as detailed or interactive as the apps outlined in this guide.

- **Cologne City Guide:** Similar to the above cited Cologne Travel Guide (only one is needed). Details on attractions in the city, shopping, dining, and tours.

- **Bonn City Guide:** Provided by the same firm which produces the Cologne City Guide. Details on the city's shopping, dining, attractions, and tours.

- **Bonn Mobile:** The city of Bonn has a complex transportation network and this app goes a long way to help understand how to use it, in addition to facilitating pass purchases.

- **DB Navigator**: This app covers train services in Germany and provides current details and routes. Train Tickets may be purchased via this app.

- **Rome2Rio**: An excellent way to research all travel options including rental cars, trains, flights, bus, and taxi. The app provides the ability to purchase tickets directly online. Covers all of Europe.

- **Google Translate:** A must if you do not know any German. This app is a tremendous help when you need to communicate with non-English speaking locals.

- **Trip Advisor**: Probably the best overall app for finding details on most hotels, restaurants, excursions, and attractions.

- **Flush**: A very helpful app which provides guidance on where to find public toilets.

~ ~ ~ ~ ~ ~

1: Cologne Overview
The Capital of Germany's Rhineland

One word can describe Cologne, a city of over one million…
<u>vibrant.</u> Okay, maybe another word or two… active and cosmo-
politan. These terms especially apply to Cologne's busy center,
the **Innenstadt.** The heart of Cologne was nearly destroyed during WWII, but it has more than simply recovered, it has thrived.

Cologne has several pedestrian shopping lanes such as the
popular Schildergasse shown here.

This "thriving" has given Cologne unflattering titles as architecturally this city is something of a hodge-podge. Since the rebuilding after WWII, any number of styles can be found in close proximity and these range from award-worthy structures to unappealing. Several resources cite the lack of urban planning as giving the city a chaotic appearance. Do not let this lack of architectural uniformity deter you. Cologne is a vibrant and fun town to visit, even if you may have minimal need to bring out your camera while visiting here.

Cologne offers visitors an interesting mix of old and new with "new" taking the upper hand. There is an enjoyable old town area to explore (Altstadt), but it is fairly small. You will not encounter a large number of areas which could be described as quaint or historic. For the most part, when exploring Cologne, expect to find a modern and busy city.

The Cologne skyline with buildings such as the Cathedral and the
Colonius Tower standing tall over the city.
Photo Source: Eckhard Henkel - Wikipedia

In geographical size, Cologne is 17 miles (27km) across, making this a moderately sized metropolitan area. This city is also well positioned between its neighbors Bonn and Düsseldorf, which has helped it grow as a center of banking and commerce. There is an interesting contrast when looking at the two neighbors of Bonn and Düsseldorf. With Bonn, it is often thought of as a part of Cologne, enough so that the two cities share resources such as a joint airport. With Düsseldorf, there is a playful rivalry with Cologne. The two towns are deemed to be bitter sports rivals and the mere mention of Düsseldorf to citizens of Cologne can bring a frown. In Cologne, they even refrain from serving the popular beers produced in Düsseldorf.

What is there to do here? Cologne and this area have a lot to offer visitors and most of them are in close proximity.

- Interested in beautiful churches? Start with the magnificent Cologne Cathedral and then head over to the nearby Great St. Martin Church.

- Maybe you enjoy contemporary architecture? Take an architectural tour to the Kranhäuser (Crane

See chapters 6, 7, 8 & 9 for details on the major attractions in and near Cologne.

The Kränhauser (Crane House)
A former industrial area near central Cologne which is now a stunning office-residential-shopping complex.
Photo Source: Rolf Heinrich-Wikimedia Commons

House) along the Rhine or ride to the top of the tower at Köln Triangle.

- History and Culture? Cologne has a delightful array of museums ranging from the Ludwig Museum with a large collection of modern art to the Wallraf-Richartz Museum with its notable artists such as Renoir and Van Gogh.

- Or maybe you just want to have some fun: Consider riding the Kölner Seilbahn cable car over the Rhine, heading to the Chocolate Museum, or the large zoo.

- Want to go shopping?: Try strolling the pedestrian shopping streets of Schildergasse and neighboring Hohe Straße. Both are not far from the cathedral and are lined with boutiques and restaurants.

In short, there are destinations here to meet every taste and preference, enough so that a stay of three or four days can easily be filled.

The Cologne Cable Car (Kölner Seilbahn)
Photo Source: Elke Wetzig-Wikimedia Commons

The Unofficial "Constitution of Cologne"

Just for fun...

Cologne has developed a fun-loving lifestyle as is apparent with their large Cologne Carnival and party atmosphere in several areas of town. To go along with this, they have crafted **"The Constitution of Cologne"** which is a bit of day-to-day wisdom with some tongue-in-cheek humor. Look for portrayals of this in the lively beer halls and restaurants in town.

	German	Loose English Translation
1	Et es wie et es	That's just the way it is.
2	Et kütt wie et küt	Whatever will be, will be.
3	Et Hätt noch immer jot Jejange	In the end, things finally work out somehow.
4	Wat fott es, es fott	Whaterver is gone, is gone
5	Nix Bliev wie et wor	Nothing remains as it was.
6	Kenne mer nit, bruche mer nit, fott domet	What we don't know, we don't need, away with it.
7	Wat wellste maache	Yield to your fate – What can you do?
8	Mache et jot ävver nit ze off	Enjoy life and stay calm.
9	Wat soll dä Quatsch	Always, first ask the meaning of life.
10	Drinkste ene met ?	Join us for a drink?
11	Do laachste dech kapott.	Laugh until it hurts.

Layout of Cologne:

A good way to begin your study of Cologne is to understand how the town is laid out and where the major transportation hubs, shopping areas, and attractions are. [4]

Cologne is defined by the presence of the Rhine River. This important waterway bisects Cologne and the terms "Right Bank" and "Left Bank" are often used to distinguish where in Cologne a location may be found.

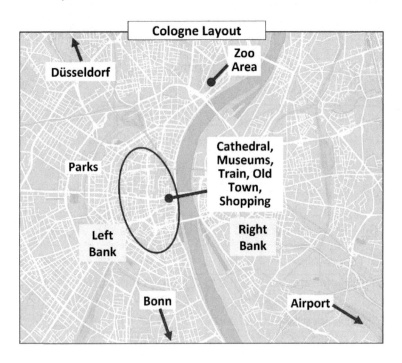

Cologne Layout

Düsseldorf

Zoo Area

Parks

Cathedral, Museums, Train, Old Town, Shopping

Left Bank

Right Bank

Bonn

Airport

---

[4] **River Orientation and some resulting confusion**: The Rhine River starts in Switzerland and is a northward flowing river emptying into the North Sea at Rotterdam. This can lead to some confusion in geographical designations. The further north you are, the more "downriver" you will be. Traveling "upriver" takes a traveler south.

The **Left Bank,** which is on the western side of the river, is the historical and business center. This is also where visitors will generally spend most of their time. Much of this area is defined by a busy road simply called "The Ring." This is an inner beltway which outlines the Innenstadt. It is a semi-circle around the heart of Cologne and is the city's most prominent street.

The **Right Bank** is more geared to day-to-day living, shopping, and industry. The three districts on the right, the 7th, 8th and 9th, were not even incorporated into the city of Cologne until the 1970s.

The Rhine River bisects the city of Cologne
Looking north. The town center and cathedral are on the Left Bank.

This city is organized into nine districts (Stadbezrikes) which are similar to arrondissements in French cities. The notable 1st district, or **Innenstadt,** is the focal point for Cologne and is where such sights as the Cologne Cathedral may be found. Six of the nine neighborhoods are on the Left Bank.

Much of the Rhine riverfront in Cologne is set aside for walking and relaxing.

It is a bit surprising when exploring Cologne to find that, given the Rhine's importance to this city, the shoreline is not heavily developed. Instead of a stretch filled with bars, office buildings, and hotels, you will find a long pedestrian promenade which is a great place to stroll or ride a bicycle. In fact, it would be easy to come to Cologne and barely spend any time along the river as most attractions are elsewhere in the city. [5]

> The Rhine River has a downside. It has frequently flooded central Cologne, causing it to be Europe's most flood-prone city.

For fun, during the weekends, there are many street fairs with vendors selling crafts and specialty foods. If you are here over a weekend, especially in the spring and summer, give it a try. There are many boat

---

[5] **Rhine River – German Spelling:** This river is Rhein in German, and this spelling is naturally used in many placename and map designations.

tour companies, especially near the cathedral, and taking one of these tours is a fun way to obtain another perspective of the city.

A relaxing aspect of Cologne is the parks. They are everywhere, small and large. One large set of parks on the left bank forms something of a semi-circle around the inner city. Across the river on the right bank is a set of parks which are often the sights for large festivals.

The Rhine River does more than simply bisect Cologne. This is also the southernmost area which is navigable by ocean-going ships. Further south (upriver) the nature of the Rhine is such that most boating traffic is limited to barges or riverboats. This is where, when following the river along its northbound path, the Rhine River enters the broad, flat area of the Rhineland.

Central Cologne - the Innenstadt:

Cologne's 1st district, or borough, is known as the Innenstadt and this is the area where most visitors will spend their time. This

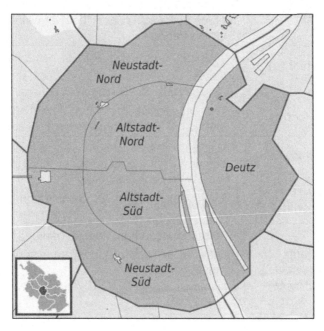

city district is divided into five sectors, with four of them being on the left bank.

Innenstadt Subsections and What is in Each One	
Subsection Name	**What is Here**
Altstadt-Nord - - - - - Old Town - North	• This is likely to be your first stop in Cologne. • Several prominent sights are here including the cathedral and Museum Ludwig • The main train station and tourist office is here as well as the old town section.
Altstadt-Süd - - - - - Old Town - South	• Several museums in this area including the Chocolate Museum and Sports and Olympics museums are here. • The waterfront area with the converted crane buildings is along the river with several restaurants.
Neustadt-Nord - - - - - New Town - North	• The northernmost subset of central Cologne. • A large park, the Stadtgarten is here. • The impressive Colonius Tower which stands tall over Cologne is here. (Closed)
Neustadt-Sud - - - - - New Town - South	• An area geared to students and small business. For the younger set, it is a good area to find bars and clubs. • The historic city gate, Sevinstorburg is here.
Deutz (This is a former town name)	• Only subsection on the right bank. • Little in the way of tourist attractions or museums. • Primarily a business area. New, modern feel.

A Few Interesting Tidbits about Cologne:

- **Beethoven began his music career here.** He was born in Bonn, the city just south of Cologne. When he was just eight, Beethoven was given the job of church organist where he gave his first concert. This was the start of his music career.

- **Cologne is the state capital.** This city of over 1 million (or over 3.6 million in the greater metropolitan area) is the capital of the German state of North Rhine Westphalia.

- **Cologne, the perfume, started here:** In 1709 a medical cure which combined alcohol and citrus was launched in the town of Cologne. It was named "Eau de Cologne" meaning simply "water from Cologne." By drinking it, many thought it would keep you from getting the plague. Now the term is generic and is no longer tied to the city of Cologne.

- **This was once a walled city:** The city boundary was formed in the early 13th century by a defensive stone wall. It was set in an arc around what is now the Inner City with fortifications lining the river. Today, all that remains are four stone gates. One of the more notable is the Severinstorburg gate, which is near the southern sector of central Cologne, and about a 1.5 mile walk from the cathedral.

- **The third tallest cathedral in the world is here** [6]: Standing at 515 feet tall / 157 meters, this 13th century structure stands proudly overlooking the city. This is one of Germany's most

---

[6] **Tallest Cathedrals:** Some sources list Cologne's cathedral as the world's tallest cathedral. Most sources cite the Cologne Cathedral in third place with the Ulm Minster Cathedral in Germany as the tallest and the Lincoln Cathedral in the U.K as the second tallest.

visited landmarks with twenty thousand visitors a day. See chapter 6 of this guide for more information.

- **Major universities are here:** Seven universities are here. The largest is the University of Cologne with over 50,000 students. Other notable universities in the city area include the Cologne University of Applied Sciences with 25,000 students.

- **The city was devastated in WWII**: As a center of industry, this was one of the most heavily bombed areas with 262 bombings, primarily by the English RAF. This killed an estimated 20,000 people and caused a great majority of citizens to evacuate the city.

The 13th century Sevinstorburg gate.
Photo Source: Raimond Spekking-Wikimedia

- **The city's name came from the Romans:** Like so much of the area, the Romans had a strong presence here. In the 1st century, the settlement was given the name Colonia Agrippina. Later the Agrippina portion was dropped, leaving Colonia as the name and, from there, the name Cologne arose. The Roman heritage is preserved in Cologne's Roman-Germanic Museum. (See chapter 7 for a guide to the area's museums).

- **Cologne has its own language**: When visiting here, you are likely to hear a variation of the German language. This localized dialect is called Kölsch. This variation on German is spoken by over a quarter of the area's population.

~ ~ ~ ~ ~ ~

2: Traveling to Cologne & Bonn

Cologne and its neighbor Bonn, have excellent transportation hubs and traveling here is generally hassle-free. Unless you are driving, the best way to come into either town is generally by train. In both cities, the primary train stations are in the heart of town and close to hotels, shopping, and attractions.

If you are arriving by air, the two cities share the Cologne Bonn airport. It is less than thirty minutes into the center of either town.

> Train travel time between Cologne and Bonn is around 20 to 25 minutes.

Travel Times to Cologne and Bonn				
From	**Travel by Train**		**Driving**	
	Cologne	**Bonn**	**Cologne**	**Bonn**
Amsterdam	3 hours+	3 hours+	2 hrs 45 min	3 hours
Brussels	1 hr, 45 min+	2 hours +	2 hrs, 20 min+	2 hours
Düsseldorf	25 min +	1 hour+	30 min	45 min
Frankfurt	1 hr, 15 min +	1 hr 30 min+	1 hr, 45 min	1 hr, 30 min

Suggested Travel Planning App:

There are several excellent online sources to help plan your transportation. One of the better firms, which is highly recommended by the author, is **"Rome2rio.com."** This firm provides an excellent website (and app) to use when trying to plan local travel to any city in Europe.

Use this service to view travel options available such as: train, flights, trams, bus, taxi, or self-drive. When choosing bus or train options, the ability to purchase tickets online is available. Schedules for trains and buses are provided with full details.

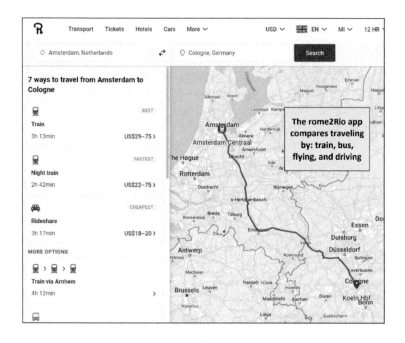

~ ~ ~ ~ ~ ~

Arriving by Train:

Trains are often the best way to travel to this area from neighboring cities and, if you have not traveled much by train in Europe, you are in for a treat.

One aspect of train travel in Germany which can be confusing is the differing identities for the various train services. At times, these services even overlap, such as the route between Cologne and Bonn. Below are some general descriptions which should help clarify, but the definitions are not perfect due to the overlaps in service.

- **S-Bahn**: Think of the "S" as identifying a suburban network. Use these trains to reach nearby towns such as Bonn or Düsseldorf. In Cologne, the S-Bahn primarily services the main train station (Köln hbf), the airport, and a limited number of other stations which are generally on the edge of town.

- **U-Bahn**: The "U" in this case can roughly be thought of as the urban network. This can be either a subway system or above ground. In Cologne, the system is also referred to as the Stadtbahn. Confusion can grow when another term, the KVB, comes up. KVB is the local transportation authority which manages trams, local trains, and the bus network.

- **DB Trains**: This is the German national railway company, the Deutsch Bahn. This includes Germany's highspeed rail network which connects most major cities.

- **Regional train services:** In addition to the three prominent service identifiers cited above, there are several regional companies, often referred to as Regional Bahns.

- **And**: Then there are tram and subway systems. Once you are in a city, including Cologne, much of your in-town transportation can be done on the local transportation system, which may also be associated with the local U-Bahn. As cited above, the agency which manages this in Cologne is the KVB, or Cologne Stadtbahn.

Cologne Train Station: You would be hard pressed to find a more convenient central train station than in Cologne. The station, the Köln Hauptbanhof (often cited as the Köln Hbf) is immediately across the street from the cathedral, the tourist office, and close to numerous museums, shops, and hotels.

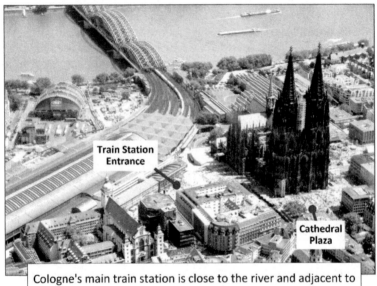

Cologne's main train station is close to the river and adjacent to the cathedral.
Photo Source: Judith Strucker - Wikipedia

When you arrive, your train will come in at a level below the main lobby. Head up one level and then, depending on your next steps, look for the signs for area transportation. The local tram and bus services stop here, so you don't have to search far to your next transportation leg. Inside the terminal are some shops and restaurants.

If you are just passing through and need a place to store your luggage while in town, there are lockers available for rent. Look for the "Left Luggage" machines on the main level.

Bonn Train Station: Bonn, like Cologne, has a very convenient central train station, the **Bonn Hauptbahnhof** (or Bonn Hbf). This station is smaller than the one in Cologne, so it is easier to find your way around.

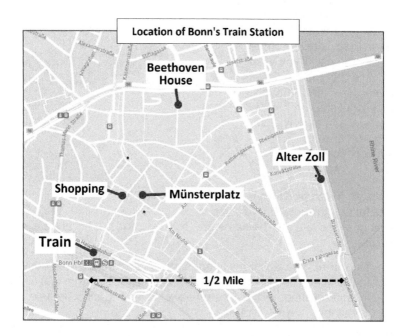

Once you arrive, simply look for the main exit and step outside. You need look no further as the city center sits directly in front of you. Head across the street and you will be on the main pedestrian shopping street, the Poststraße. From here it is less than a five-minute walk to the large Münsterplatz plaza which is the heart of the town. Go another five minutes and you come upon the Bee-thoven House. (See chapter 13 for details on the attractions in Bonn).

Flying into Cologne and Bonn:

Cologne and Bonn share an airport which is equidistant between the two cities on the right (east) side of the Rhine River.

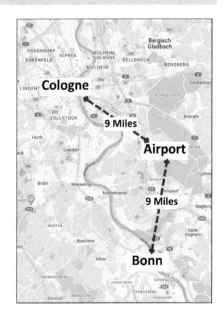

The Köln-Bonn Airport (CGN) has flights from many European cities, so finding a direct flight to here from within Europe is easy to do. If you wish to view a complete list of departures and arrivals, they are listed on the airport website at: **www.Cologne-Bonn-Airport.com.**

Airport Transportation:
Guidelines for obtaining ground transportation into either central Cologne or Bonn are the same and, in both cases, it is very easy to do.

- Light Rail: The S-Bahn system services the airport from both towns in addition to regional train companies. The train station is underground, below the arrivals and departures area. Reservations are not needed for this train service.

- Bus: In addition to the city buses, there is an express bus service. Check **www.SWB-BusundBahn.de** for details.

> **Fun Fact:**
> The Cologne airport is set up to operate as an emergency landing site for NASA shuttles if need arises. It is the only runway in Germany which can do this.

- **Taxi or Private Car**: If your first destination is a hotel, consider taking a taxi or similar service as this greatly reduces hassle and you arrive directly at your lodging. For most locations in either town, the ride will be just 15 to 20 minutes.

In addition to taxis, several services are available and may be booked in advance including:

- Sixt – **www.Sixt.com**

- Welcome Pickups – **www.WelcomePickups.com**

~ ~ ~ ~ ~ ~

3: When to Visit

Cologne and the Rhineland have a four-season climate. The number of visitors to here naturally ebb-and-flows with the changing seasons. There are some noteworthy exceptions as major events can bring in huge crowds in the winter.

> Almost any time between early May to the end of October is a good time to explore this area.

If you are crowd-averse but still want comfortable weather, the best times to visit the area are in the Spring and Fall. If you want to come for a lively party atmosphere, then consider coming for the Christmas Markets, or to the Cologne Carnival, one of Europe's biggest parties.

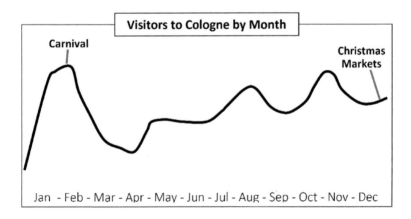

Visitors to Cologne by Month

Carnival

Christmas Markets

Jan - Feb - Mar - Apr - May - Jun - Jul - Aug - Sep - Oct - Nov - Dec

Some Seasonal Considerations:

For starters, a quick summary of average temperatures and precipitation may be beneficial.

Average Area Climate by Month				
Month		**Avg High**	**Avg Low**	**Avg Precip**
Jan	☹	43 F / 6 C	32 F /0 C	2.4 inches
Feb	☹	45 F / 7 C	32 F /0 C	2.1 inches
Mar	😐	53 F /11 C	36 F /2 C	2.2 inches
Apr	😐	61 F /16 C	40 F /5 C	1.9 inches
May	☺	68 F /20 C	47 F /8 C	2.4 inches
Jun	☺	73 F /23 C	52 F /11 C	3.4 inches
Jul	☺	77 F /25 C	56 F /13 C	3.4 inches
Aug	☺	76 F /25 C	55 F /13 C	3.3 inches
Sep	☺	69 F / 20 C	50 F /10 C	2.6 inches
Oct	😐	59 F /15 C	44 F /7 C	2.6 inches
Nov	😐	50 F /10 C	38 F / 4 C	2.5 inches
Dec	☹	44 F / 7 C	34 F /1 C	2.7 inches

Winter: As cited earlier, this is truly an area with four seasons so it will come as little surprise to learn that winter in the Rhineland can be bitterly cold with frequent rain or snow. Curiously, Cologne is at its most crowded in February when the noteworthy Cologne Carnival occurs. Information on the area's top events is later in this chapter. Bottom-line, if you come here in the winter, bundle-up.

Cologne's Cathedral in the Winter

Spring: Late Spring is a good time to visit here. Rain in the Spring in this area is not extremely different from other times of the year (See table on previous page). This is a good time to visit without being inundated by crowds, especially when visiting the major sights such as the Cathedral and Ludwig Museum. Rates for lodging will be low as well.

Summer: The city is pleasantly popular during the summer. This means that there are enough visitors to make it feel lively, but not so many as to be overwhelming. Prices are up for lodging, but all tours are in full swing. This is a great time to take a riverboat tour or a walk along the Rhine River.

Do what the locals do during summer in Cologne, relax at a park along the Rhine.
Photo Source: Janko Hoener - Wikimedia Commons

Fall: For many, this is the best time to visit here, and it tends to be the most popular time of year for visitors. The weather tends to be favorable, and tours are operating. Lodging rates will be high in the Fall. Bottom line, the fall can be relatively crowded, but it is still one of the best times to visit Cologne and the Rhineland.

Festivals and Major Events:

Every city has a full array of events ranging from small festivals to massive events. Cologne is no exception. If you wish to view a list of all the city's events, check out **www.AllEvents.In/Cologne**

There are two major events each year in Cologne which stand out above the rest in popularity. The city's Christmas Markets and the huge Cologne Carnival. Both occur during the winter season.

Cologne Christmas Market: Considered by many to be one Germany's best Christmas market cities. It dates back to 1820. Cologne has a collection of several markets spread throughout the town with the largest and most noted located just outside of the cathedral. The Cathedral market area is covered by lights which give it a warm and inviting appearance. The Christmas markets in Cologne typically run from mid-November to either Christmas or New Years, but they do vary slightly.

Dates: Typically, the dates will run from mid-November to just before Christmas. A few of the markets stay open until the end of the year. The best website to check current schedules is **www.Cologne.de** - then go to the events page.

The Cathedral Christmas Market. One of several in Cologne.
Photo Source: Superbass - Wikimedia Commons

Leading Cologne Christmas Markets		
Market	**German Name**	**Where**
Cathedral Christmas Market	Weihnachts-markt am Dom	Cathedral Plaza

Leading Cologne Christmas Markets		
Market	German Name	Where
(This is the largest market)		
Nicholas Village Christmas Market (A quaint Christmas village setting)	Nikolausdorf am Rudolfplatz	Hanen Gate / Hahnentorburg Just west of the town center.
Cologne Harbor Christmas Market (River/Nautical themed Christmas Market)	Kölner Hafen Weihnachts-markt	Adjacent to the Chocolate Museum
House Elves Fairytale Christmas Market (Fairytale village atmosphere)	Heinzels Wintermärchen	Heumarkt Large plaza a few blocks south of the cathedral

Cologne Carnival / Kölner Karneval: This event is huge and is said to be one of the largest parties in Europe and is often compared to the New Orleans Mardi Gras. In 2022, it was attended by over 1.5 million people.

This six-day event runs for the week which ends on Ash Wednesday of each year, typically in late February. It is known for the many parades, outlandish costumes, and the unending flow of beer. If you come, plan on dressing up in costume. Any costume, the crazier the better, will do.

If you like parties, this is the place to be. If you are planning on coming to Cologne primarily to admire the cathedral and museums, this is the time to avoid Cologne.

Details for this event may be found on the Cologne Tourism website: **www.Cologne-Tourism.com - t**hen go to the section titled "See & Experience."

~ ~ ~ ~ ~ ~

4: Cologne & Bonn Discount Cards

If you will be staying overnight in the area and are devoting multiple days to attractions, such as area museums or river boat tours, you should consider purchasing an area discount pass.

Both Cologne and Bonn have their own local passes. Each provides a mix of free admissions and discounts to local sights and even restaurants.

These passes provide value and convenience **IF** you plan on visiting multiple museums, taking several trips on local transportation, or area tours.

One fun side-effect of purchasing this sort of pass is they often lead you to area attractions, such as specialty museums, of which you might not have been aware.

The Köln Card:

In Cologne, the Köln Card is more of a set of discounts than free admission to attractions. A benefit of this plan is it keeps the price down compared to the plans in many other cities which have free admissions, but the cost of the cards can be quite high.

Website for full details: **www.Cologne-Tourism.com**. Then follow the icon and link to the Köln Card.

Options Available: The cards are available for 24 or 48 hours. This timing is measured from when it is first used. The two other variations are single passes or group passes. If you purchase a group pass, it covers up to 5 people.

Where to Purchase: Ideally, if your schedule allows, you should wait to go to the tourist office which is adjacent to the cathedral. By purchasing it there, the office personnel can also provide helpful maps and advice. The provided map will highlight all the sights and activities which are covered.

Other resellers include many area hotels, especially the larger chains, and several online resellers such as: **www.Civitatis.com**, or the local transportation service at **www.Kvb.com**.

Köln Card Pricing As of mid-2023		
Duration	**Individual Rate**	**Group Rate**
24 Hours	€ 9	€ 19
48 Hours	€ 18	€ 38

What is Included: One of the benefits of this program is free use of the local transportation system including buses and trams. In addition to this, numerous discounts on museums, shops, and restaurants are included. Example of attractions and businesses providing benefits to card holders include:

- Transportation: Free use of local buses and trams. Discounts on bicycle rentals.

- Cologne Cathedral: Discounted admission to the cathedral and accompanying museum.

- Museums: Discounts ranging from 20% to 50% on area museums including such popular destinations as: the Chocolate Museum; Museum Ludwig; and the Fragrance Museum.

- Tours and Sightseeing: Discounts ranging from 15 to 50% on several tour offerings including the local Hop-On Bus, TV Backstage Tour, and Guided City Tour.

- Restaurants & Shops: Several area restaurants and stores, including the Tourist Office, offer discounts ranging from 10% to 20% to Köln Card holders.

The Bonn Regional Welcome Card:

In Cologne, the Bonn Welcome Card (Bonn Regio in German) is a 24-hour card which is valid from its first use. The benefits range from free admission on local transportation and some museums to discounts in numerous area museums and attractions.

The website for this discount card is: **www.Bonn-Region.de.**

There are three geographical variations available for this card and the cost increases with the area covered.

- Welcome Card Bonn – covers attractions just in the city of Bonn.

- Welcome Card Bonn Plus – expanded coverage to include attractions in many area towns.

- Welcome Card VRS – includes everything in the Welcome Card Bonn Plus, and travel on the regional transportation service.

In addition to the geographical variations, these passes are available for individuals or families. A family pass covers two adults and up to three children.

Bonn Welcome Card Pricing As of mid-2023 – 24-Hour Passes		
Duration	**Individual Rate**	**Family Rate**
Welcome Card Bonn	€ 10	€ 19
Welcome Card Bonn Plus	€ 14	€ 26
Welcome Card VRS	€ 24	€ 49

Where to purchase: The passes are available either directly from the Bonn tourist office or their website at **www.Bonn-Region.de.**

What is Included:

- Transportation: Free use of local buses, trams and ferries with the VRS version. Or, for fun, ride Germany's oldest cog railway, the Drachenfels, at a discounted rate.

- Free City Map: The Tourist Office provides free, detailed city maps to holders of the Bonn Welcome Card.

- Museums: Discounts ranging from 10% to 50% on area museums including the Beethoven House and Bonn Art Museum.

- Tours and Shows: Discounts on the Bonn City Tour bus, and several shows such as the Beethoven Orchestra.

- Cologne Discounts: Discounts on several popular Cologne attractions such as the Chocolate Museum and Fragrance Museum.

- Restaurants & Shops: Several restaurants and stores offer discounts or perks ranging from a free beer with your meal to discounts on purchases.

Get discounts on Germany's oldest cog railway with the Bonn Welcome Card

Photo Source: Tohma - Wikemedia Commons

~ ~ ~ ~ ~ ~

5: Transportation in Cologne

Learning how to find your way around a new city can be daunting. The good news/bad news situation with Cologne is that it has a comprehensive network of transportation options and learning it can be intimidating at first.

A big plus to the transportation system in and around Cologne is that almost every destination is easily reachable either on foot or by local transportation. The need for rental cars or taxis is rare.

In central Cologne, most destinations are within easy walking distance, but some sights are a greater walk than most of us want to endure. Taking the local transportation is a good idea.

In this area you have the following transportation options:

- Trams and Subways
- Local Railways – U-Bahn, S-Bahn and regional rail.
- Bicycle Rental
- Hop-On/Hop-Off Tour Bus

Cologne's light rail system is a mixture of above-ground and underground lines.
Photo Source: Kurt Rasmussen-Wikimedia Commons

Getting Around on Foot:

Exploring central Cologne on foot, in the area known as Innenstadt, is generally easy. For starters, it is flat and there are few cobblestone streets to hamper mobility-impaired individuals.

Some locations such as the zoo or the botanical gardens are out a ways, but the main train station, old town, the cathedral, and most destinations are easy to reach on foot.

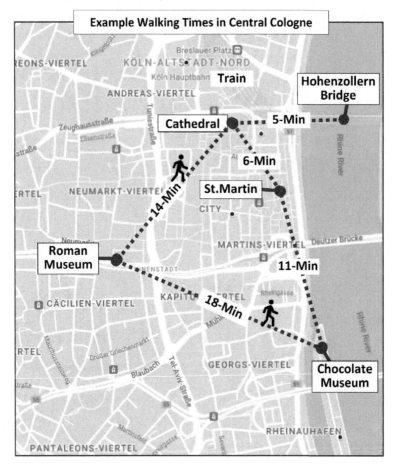

Example Walking Times in Central Cologne

Trams, Subways & Buses:

By any measure, the transportation network in Cologne is excellent and comprehensive. It is also complex which generates an initial learning curve (or a bit of trepidation).

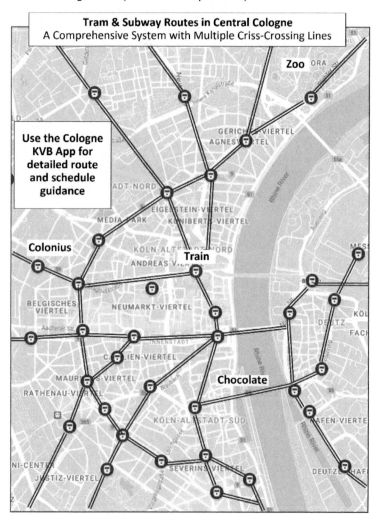

Tram & Subway Routes in Central Cologne
A Comprehensive System with Multiple Criss-Crossing Lines

One bit of good news is de-tailed route boards are present at every stop. Still, **having the app at hand can be very helpful**, especially as it will provide specific details on which route to take to reach your desired destination.

At first, it seems like there are two separate networks. One for above-ground trams and another for below-ground subways. In actuality, this is the same set of lines as one route is likely to be above or below ground depending on where you are in the city.

Often this is referred to as the Cologne Stadtbahn, but the formal name is **Kölner Verkehrs-Betriebe,** or simply **KVB.** This network includes area bicycle rentals in addition to the tram and bus system.

Full details on the system and rates may be found at: **www.KVB.Koeln.**

Trams and buses are included in the **Köln Card**, area discount program.

Pricing & Tickets: First, the easy part, acquiring tickets. Ticket machines are available at every tram and subway stop and they are also on most train cars. Purchases may be made with cash (Euro coins) or credit cards. Another good way to purchase your tickets is through the KVB app.

Now, the complex part…ticket options. The price structure is daunting and there are many variables including: time frame, distance of travel, where you travel, and age of the traveler. TIP: If you are just traveling within central Cologne, consider purchasing either a 4-Ticket pass or a short-distance pass for each one-way trip.

VRS-TICKET-ÜBERSICHT

Tickets & Preisstufen	K	1a	1b	2a	2b	3	4	5	6	7
Einzel- und 4erTickets										
EinzelTicket Erwachsene	2,10	2,60	3,20	3,20	4,20	5,60	8,60	12,50	15,50	19,00
EinzelTicket Kinder (6–14 J.)	1,00	1,40	1,70	1,70	2,10	2,70	3,90	5,40	7,40	8,90
4erTicket Erwachsene	8,40	10,40	12,80	12,80	16,80	22,40	34,40	50,00	62,00	76,00
4erTicket Kinder (6-14 J.)	4,00	5,60	6,80	6,80	8,40	10,80	15,60	21,60	29,60	35,60
4erTicket MobilPass		6,00	7,10	7,10	9,90	12,60	19,60	28,80		
24Stunden Tickets										
24StundenTicket 1 Person		6,30	7,70	7,70	10,10	13,40	17,20	25,00	28,40	31,00
24StundenTicket 5 Personen		11,60	15,20	15,20	19,10	22,90	30,70	42,10	46,70	49,10
ZeitTickets Erwachsene										
WochenTicket		22,00	30,40	30,40	38,10	46,20	68,20	83,30	98,10	113,10
MonatsTicket		84,40	114,00	114,00	143,70	173,60	259,30	313,30	331,30	351,40
MonatsTicket im Abo		70,80	92,90	92,90	117,50	141,70	209,60	251,10	262,30	276,20
MonatsTicket MobilPass		34,50	45,80	45,80	53,00	66,70	76,60	92,60		
MonatsTicket MobilPass im Abo		27,90	37,10	37,10	42,80	52,40	62,00	74,90		
Formel9Ticket		60,60	81,10	81,10	93,00	114,50	136,50	164,70		
Formel9Ticket im Abo		50,10	67,00	67,00	76,80	94,00	112,00	135,40		
Aktiv60Ticket (Abo)		46,40	62,00	62,00	69,60	84,50	100,50	117,70	131,60	146,80
ZeitTickets Schüler/Azubis										
MonatsTicket		65,50	83,70	83,70	106,10	128,20	191,00	230,90	249,50	269,00
PrimaTicket		57,30	74,90	74,90	94,80	114,30	168,90	202,50		
StarterTicket (Abo)		57,30	74,90	74,90	94,80	114,30	168,90	202,50	212,40	223,30
AzubiTicket (Abo)					66,50					
Zuschläge 1. Klasse										
Einzelfahrt		1,30	1,60	1,60	2,10	2,80	4,30	6,30	7,80	9,50
Woche		11,00	15,20	15,20	19,10	23,10	34,10	41,70	49,10	56,60
Monat		42,20	57,00	57,00	71,90	86,80	129,70	156,70	165,70	175,70
Jahr (Monatsrate)		35,40	46,50	46,50	58,80	70,90	104,80	125,60	131,20	138,10
Schnellbuszuschläge Linie SB60										
Einzelfahrt Erwachsene					3,60					
Einzelfahrt Kinder (6–14 J.)					1,80					
Woche					18,60					
Monat					61,60					
Jahr (Monatsrate)					49,90					
Zuschlag Fahrradmitnahme										
FahrradTicket					3,20					
Monat					42,20					
AnschlussTicket										
Einzelfahrt VRS-AnschlussTicket				4,40 (gilt nur in Verbindung mit VRS-ZeitTickets)						

The KVB Price Matrix is complex with many options.

Ⓢ Diese VRS-Tickets gibt es auch als HandyTicket – mit einem Preisvorteil von 3 %.

Ⓞ Diese VRS-Tickets gibt es auch als OnlineTicket – mit einem Preisvorteil von 3 %.

Kinder unter 6 Jahren und Hunde fahren grundsätzlich kostenlos mit.

Maßgeblich für die genauen Preise und Leistungen aller Tickets sind die Beförderungsbedingungen Nahverkehr NRW und die Tarifbestimmungen des VRS, die Sie unter **vrs.de** finden.

Alle Preise in EUR, gültig ab 01.05.2023

Bike Share Service:

Cologne is a bike-friendly city with level land and many bike lanes. Like many European cities, renting a bike to explore the town and area is simple. Consider, for example, taking a leisurely bike ride along the Rhine up to the zoo area, or heading out to the parks which surround much of the city.

KVB Rental Bicycle Locations Are Throughout Cologne

Many bicycle rental agencies are available and some firms even provide specialty bikes or bike tours. For casual bike rentals, consider using the KVB-Rad Service. This service works in association with KVB, the area's transportation network of trams and buses. It is managed by NextBike which provides similar bike share services throughout Europe.

Using this program is simple, but it does **require that you use either the Next Bike app, or the KVB Transportation app**.

Once you have the app downloaded, you will need to set it up with your personal information including credit card details.

Then, with the app setup, simply locate an available bike near you, follow the instructions at the bike stand, then enjoy your day. You may return the bicycle to any station with an available position. The apps show which bike stands have available bikes and openings to return a bike.

Website for full details: **www.KVB-Rad.de**

Once you rent a bike, you will be charged one Euro for every fifteen minutes, up to a maximum of 15 Euros per day. There is an extra fee to return the bike to some of the further-out locations which are referred to as flex zones within their system.

City Tour / Hop-On Bus:

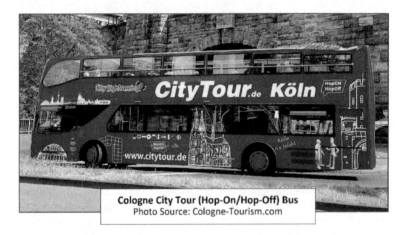

Cologne City Tour (Hop-On/Hop-Off) Bus
Photo Source: Cologne-Tourism.com

If you wish to obtain an understanding of Cologne, beyond just the top museums, consider taking the City Tour Bus (also referred to as the Hop-On/Hop-Off bus).

Most cities offer this type of tour and there are several advantages to them including the ability to

There are Two different types of "Hop-On" Tours in Cologne.

A double-decker bus and a small trolley service both provide hop-on transportation here.

easily view much of the city and the ability to "hop-off" at your leisure.

In Cologne, this bus service has 14 stops along the route which range from major attractions such as the Chocolate Museum or Zoo, to lesser stops such as area plazas or the sports arena.

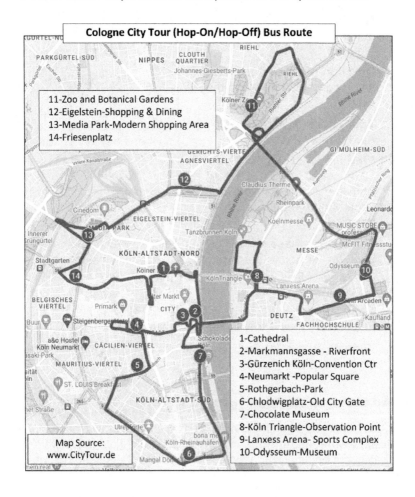

Cologne City Tour (Hop-On/Hop-Off) Bus Route

11-Zoo and Botanical Gardens
12-Eigelstein-Shopping & Dining
13-Media Park-Modern Shopping Area
14-Friesenplatz

1-Cathedral
2-Markmannsgasse - Riverfront
3-Gürzenich Köln-Convention Ctr
4-Neumarkt -Popular Square
5-Rothgerbach-Park
6-Chlodwigplatz-Old City Gate
7-Chocolate Museum
8-Köln Triangle-Observation Point
9-Lanxess Arena- Sports Complex
10-Odysseum-Museum

Map Source:
www.CityTour.de

Details on the City-Tour Hop-On program include:

- **Bus:** Look for red or yellow buses with the bold City Tour logo. Both color buses run the same route. These are double-decker buses which can accommodate wheelchairs on the lower level.

- **Number of stops**: 14. The starting point is next to the cathedral.

- **Duration of trip:** 90 minutes, if you do not get off along the way.

- **When does it operate**: Early April to late October.

- **Frequency of buses**: Every 30 minutes. If you start out from the Cathedral, the bus departs on the hour and half-hour.

> **Rhine River Boat Tour**
>
> The City Tour Company also operates a boat tour on the Rhine. Discounts are provided when both tour types are purchased together.

- **Tickets purchase sites**: The City Tour (Hop-On Bus) pass is good for 24 hours, starting from first usage. Tickets may be purchased on the bus, via the website, or from other resellers such as Viator.com.

- **Cost:** As of mid-2023, the rates are: € 18 for adults and € 5 for children ages 4 to 13. (Rates are subject to change).

- **Website**: **www.CityTour.de** – then go to the page for the Cologne City Tour.

Wolters Bimmelbahnen / Hop-On Trolley:

Another service which provides a riding tour service is the quaint **Wolters Bimmelbahnen**. This is a small, train-like service which takes riders on different "express" circuits and stays near the center of the city. The ability to hop-on or off is limited as these are essentially direct trips to the end point, but they meander through interesting areas of town and even along the river.

Website for this program is: **www.BimmelBahnen.com**.

Routes: There are three different routes, which have substantial overlap.

Chocoloate Express: Starts
near the cathedral. It travels
through the Old Town area
(Alstadt) with the endpoint at
the Chocolate Museum which
is slightly south from the heart
of town. The one-way trip from the cathedral to the museum takes
roughly 25 minutes.

Zoo Express: This starts at the same place near the cathedral but
heads north instead of south. The endpoint is the Cologne Zoo
and Botanical Garden. Combined passes which include the cable
car over the Rhine are available. This route takes 15 to 20 minutes
each way and a round-trip will take a bit under an hour.

Christmas Market Express: There are several different Christmas Market locations in Cologne each year and this route carries
visitors to the major markets, and in a warm train instead of having
to travel in the winter weather. This route naturally only operates
when the Christmas Markets are open in the winter.

Frequency: The Zoo and Chocolate Museum routes leave every
thirty minutes while the Christmas Market route departs every 15
minutes.

Cost: The rates for mid-2023 are €10 for adults for a round-trip on
either the Chocolate or Zoo routes. Child fare is half of this. If you
have a Köln Card, there is a modest discount. All rates are subject
to change.

~ ~ ~ ~ ~ ~

6: The Cologne Cathedral
The Kölner Dom

Cologne's cathedral, the **Kölner Dom**, is the city's most popular attraction and icon. Over six million people visit this UNESCO World Heritage site annually and it is one of Germany's top attractions.

This is an active religious structure, but it is open to visit most hours and days. It is also very easy to reach as it is just steps from Cologne's main train station. Visitors may not only tour the main hall, the nave, but also climb up to the towers or go down under the church to visit the treasury chambers.

Cathedral Interior
Photo Source: Thomas Robbin - Wikipedia

Cathedral Website

Full details on current hours, tours, church history, and features check the following:

www.Koelner-dom.de

In preparation for your visit, the following background information may be beneficial

Some Notable Facts:

- The church took almost 630 years to build. Construction began in 1248 and it was completed in 1880. Part of the reason for the lengthy period was a construction pause of over 230 years. This pause was the mixture of influences from the Reformation and changing finances of the city brought on by different trade routes which by-passed Cologne.

- The original goal for building the church was to create a shrine for the Relics of the Magi, otherwise known as the Shrine of the Three Kings. This is currently on display in the church. Prior to being brought to Cologne, these relics had been in Milan until the twelfth century.

Curious Fact

The two towers are not the same height. The southern tower, (closest to the train station) is 2 inches shorter.

- When the church was finished in 1880, it was the tallest building in the world, with the two towers reaching upwards 515 feet (157 meters). It lost this distinction just ten years later when the Ulm Germany Cathedral was built. The Cologne Cathedral is still the largest Gothic church in Northern Europe.

- Over 300,000 tons of stone were used in the construction. When visiting it, the massive size of 472 feet (144 meters) long by 282 feet (86 meters) wide is evidence of this.

- The primary cathedral chamber, the nave, is 142.2 feet tall (43.4 m) and like most Gothic cathedrals, it is built in the shape of a Latin Cross. It covers 86,111 square feet (8,000 sq meters).

- During the French Revolution in the 1790s, the city was occupied by the French and for several years the nave of the church was used as a stable and hay barn.

- During WWII, the cathedral was bombed repeatedly causing heavy ruins. Restoration work began at the close of the war and it was reopened in 1956.

Layout of the Cathedral & Some Highlights:

Numerous treasures, old and new, are present within the main chambers. They start with the entrance and continue on to the valts below and the bells above you.

Some of the features to watch for include:

Entrance: The primary entrance is known as **Petersportal**. It is the only entrance which was built, in part, in the Middle Ages. The other entrances were all put in place in the 19th century, close to

Petersportal Entrance to the Cologne Cathedral

the date the cathedral was completed in 1880.

The Shrine of the Three Kings: Also referred to as the Epiphany

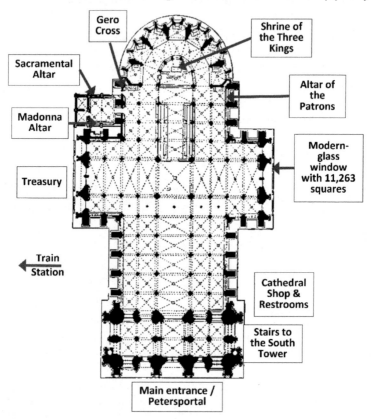

Shrine or the Tomb of the Magi. This shrine which is believed to contain the remains of the three magi, or Three Wise Men, was the reason the cathedral was built.

The shrine came to Cologne in the 12th century from Milan. Covered in gold, it is shaped like a church and is adorned with several large jewels. This shrine was opened in 1864, near the time when the cathedral was completed, and it was proven to contain bones and garments. In size, it is over seven feet long and five feet high.

The Shrine of the Three Kings
Photo Source: Welleschik - Wikimedia Commons

Gero Cross (Gero-Kreuz): Carved in Oak in the 10th century, this six-foot tall cross is the oldest known crucifix north of the Alps. It is partially gilded and is the earliest known depiction of a dead Christ on the cross. The figure is life-size and the cross is over six-feet tall. It may be found in the cathedral in its own small chapel, or sacristy.

The Gero Cross

Altar of the Patrons: Also referred to as the Altar of Patron Saints or Dombild Altarpiece. Built in the 15th century, this three-panel painting (a Triptych) done in the Gothic

Cologne style was first built in honor of the city council and placed in a different, smaller church.

Milan Madonna Altar: Also known as the Mailänder Madonna. This is a 13th century wood sculpture which depicts the Virgin Mary with infant Jesus. It is the oldest Madonna artifact in the cathedral and is thought by many to have miraculous powers.

Mosaic Glass Window: With so many ancient treasures in the cathedral, it can come as a surprise to find that one of the larger decorative windows was recently created.

The Cologne Cathedral Window on the south-facing side was done by noted artist Gerhard Richter and completed in 2007. It is in an abstract style and has 11,263 colored glass squares.

The Gerhard Richter Window

Visiting the South Tower:

If you are in good shape, consider going to the top of the south tower or to the Belfry. The trek up the tower is a climb of 533 steps up to the 100-meter level. The roundtrip will take roughly 60 to 90 minutes.

Tickets are required and, given the small group size, advance reservations are highly recommended. Book through the cathedral website at: **www.DomFuehrugen-Koeln.de.** There is a modest fee to go up the tower.

Hours vary slightly by the season with a typical opening time of 9AM and closing between 4PM to 6PM depending on the time of year. Guided tours are available.

View of The Rhine and Cologne from the Cathedral Tower
Photo Source: Dronepicr - Wikimedia Commons

The Treasury:

While a trip to the tower takes you to the upper reaches of the cathedral, consider also going below into the vaulted cellars to visit the Cathedral Treasury. This is a facility housing items dating from the 4th century up until the 20th century.

An interesting aspect of this collection is that it is not really a museum. All items here are still in use by the church. The collection includes ancient chalices, vestments, relics of the Three Kings, and ancient Christian art.

Just like a visit to the tower, there is a fee to visit this museum and discounted, combination tickets are available. Fees are modest.

The museum is on the north, or railroad, side of the building. Normal hours are 10AM to 6PM.

Helpful Information for a Visit:

Visitor Restrictions: Touring is not allowed when mass is in session. In general, hours open to touring are between 10AM and 5PM Monday to Saturday and 1PM to 5PM on Sunday. If you wish to view the schedule of upcoming masses, visit: **www.Koelnerdom.de.**

Fees: There is no fee to enter the cathedral nor are reservations needed. There are fees to go up into the tower or visit The Treasury.

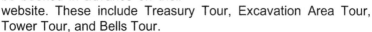

App: An app is available for Apple and Android devices which is specific to the cathedral. It provides mass times, tour hours, details on the works of art, and spiritual thoughts.

Tours: The church provides several guided tours which may be booked in advance on their website. These include Treasury Tour, Excavation Area Tour, Tower Tour, and Bells Tour.

Cameras and Cell Phones: Photography is allowed. If you are using a cellphone, the church asks that it be kept in silent mode as this is a house of worship. Drones are not allowed inside the cathedral, nor may they be used from the tower.

Clothing: Guests are asked to dress in accordance with this being a house of worship. No short skirts or offensive garments, please.

~ ~ ~ ~ ~ ~

7: Cologne Points of Interest

The Cologne Cathedral is far from the only attraction here. Points of interest range from world-class museums to enjoyable shopping areas or plazas to kick back and watch the world go by.

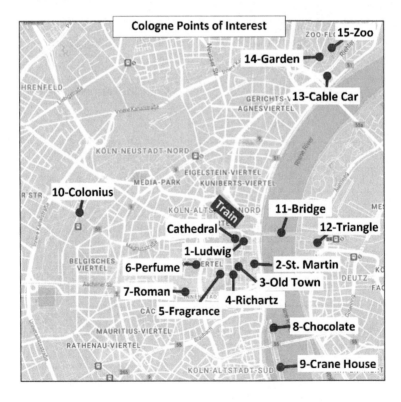

This chapter provides guidance on fifteen suggested destinations within Cologne which are outlined in the table below.

Cologne Attractions (See map on previous page)		
Map Code	**Type**	**Name**
1	Art Museum	Museum Ludwig
2	Church	Great St. Martin Church
3	Plazas & Shopping	Old Town Area
4	Fine Arts Museum	Wallraf-Richartz Museum
5	Fragrance Museum	Farina Duftmuseum
6	Perfume Store	Dufthaus 4711 Perfume
7	Museum	Römish-Germanisches
8	Museum	Cologne Chocolate Museum
9	Business Park	Crane House Complex
10	Observation Tower	Colonius Turm-CLOSED
11	Bridge w/Love Locks	Hohenzollern Bridge
12	Observation Tower	Köln Triangle
13	Cable Car	Kölner-Seilbahn
14	Botanical Garden	Flora and Botanischer Garten
15	Zoo	Cologne Zoological Garden

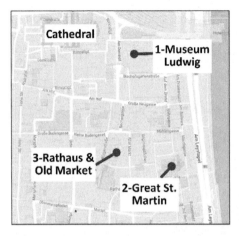

Old Town Area Points of Interest: Cologne's "Old Town" is a popular area to explore and includes several attractions cited in the above table including the impressive Great St. Martin Church and plazas lined with shops such as the Rathausplatz. Each of the attractions outlined here are within an easy walk of the cathedral.

1-Museum Ludwig:

Adjacent to the cathedral is a large modern art museum, the Museum Ludwig.

The name comes from Peter Ludwig, a chocolate magnate, who provided the initial endowment.

Today, it is considered to be a major destination

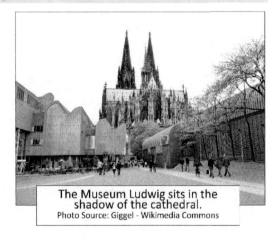

The Museum Ludwig sits in the shadow of the cathedral.
Photo Source: Giggel - Wikimedia Commons

for lovers of modern art. Displays range from expressionism to pop art and includes the work of famous artists such as Picasso and Warhol. There are also large photographic exhibits.

Website: **www.Museum-Ludwig.de**

<u>Fees:</u> The 2023 adult rate is €12, plus added fees for special exhibits. Köln Card holders will receive a 20% discount.

<u>Hours:</u> Normal hours: Tuesday to Sunday 10AM to 6PM, closed on Monday.

2-Great St. Martin Church / Groß Sankt Martin:

Great St. Martin Church
Photo Source: DeWp - Wikimedia Commons

Just a six-minute walk south from the cathedral is another impressive church, the Great St. Martin Church which was built in the Romanesque style in 1250. An interesting timeline note is the cathedral's construction started in 1248, just about the time construction on Great St. Martin was coming to completion.

Construction started in 1150 so, relatively speaking, the construction timeframe of 100 years was fairly short. There had been another church on this site but a major fire in Cologne in 1150 destroyed that building and much of the city at the time.

The interior is defined as minimalistic as the array of artwork and statuary is limited. The church towers stand 246 feet tall, (50 meters).

Great St. Martin Interior
Photo Source: Elke Wetzig - Wikipedia

Address: An Groß St. Martin 9, 50667 Köln

Fees: There are no fees to enter and view the church.

Hours: Normal hours: Tuesday to Sunday 10AM to 7:30PM, closed on Monday.

Nearby: The church is next to the riverfront on the eastern side, and less than a block from the Rathaus and Alter Market.

3-Old Town / Rathaus / Fish Market / Hay Market:

The area close to St. Martin Church is often referred to as Old Town. There are several plazas here in addition to the historic town hall, the Rathaus. If you come during the Christmas season, each of the plazas has its own market and unique character. This area is flat and easy to explore on foot. Some of the highlights include:

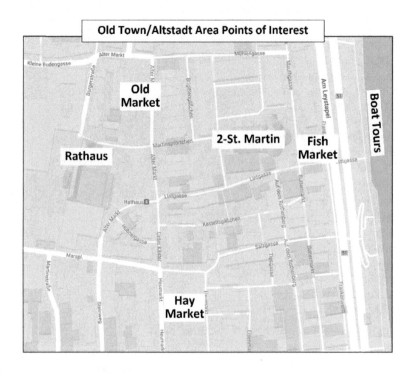

Old Town/Altstadt Area Points of Interest

Rathaus: This is an historic city hall and one of the more photo-worthy buildings in the area. It borders two squares, the Rathausplatz and Alter Markt. This was built in the 14th century and is Germany's oldest city hall. One of the highlights is the bell tower or glockenspiel which has 48 bronze bells and rings four times each day.

Old Market Square / Alter Mkt: An attractive open square lined with shops and restaurants. The square dates to the 10th century and provides excellent photo opportunities, including the Rathaus. The subway stops here at the "Rathaus" station which is convenient to both the Old Market and neighboring Hay Market squares.

Fish Market / Fischmarkt: This is, for many visitors who come by river cruise, the first place they will come to in Cologne. A small but attractive square which sits between the river and St. Martin Church. The row of colorful buildings facing the river are quaint and the area is lined with restaurants. During Christmas, this is one of the more popular market areas. The adjacent riverfront is where many of the enjoyable Rhine boat tours may be found.

Cologne's Old Market / Alter Markt
Photo Source: Raimond Spekking - Wikimedia Commons

Hay Market / Neumarkt: A large square which sits two blocks south of St. Martin Church. It is often the site of fairs and markets. If you have a car, there is a large parking area under this plaza. The city's largest Christmas market is held here. Like the other squares nearby, this is a good area to come to enjoy a variety of restaurants and bars. It is well known for its breweries.

4-Wallraf-Richartz Museum:

Tucked away on a quiet street just south of the Rathaus and Old Market Square is a fine arts museum with an impressive collection. The focus of the collections is on fine art with works from the Medieval period up to the 19th Century.

The collections include works from such masters as Van Gogh, Renoir, Gaugin, and many others. Explore the expansive Baroque

Van Gogh's *Langlois Bridge in Arles* is among the works on display here.

collection which includes works by Rubens and Frans Hals. The Impressionist galleries include Monet, Pissarro, and Morisot.

Website: **www.Wallraf.Museum**

Address: Obenmarspforten 40, 50667 Köln

Subway: The closest subway/tram station is Rathaus, a short 3-minute walk east from the museum.

Fees: The 2023 adult rate is €8 and discounts are provided to holders of the Köln Card.

Hours: Normal hours: Tuesday to Sunday 10AM to 6PM, closed on Monday.

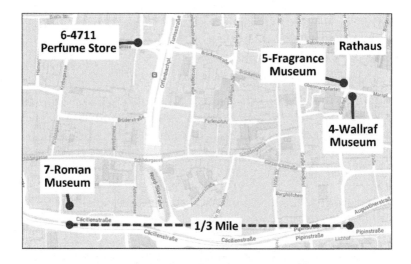

5-Fragrance Museum / Farina Duftmuseum:

With Cologne being at the historical epicenter of, well, cologne, it is not surprising to find notable destinations which focus on the history of Eau de Cologne.

The Fragrance Museum, or Farina Duftmuseum, sits across the street from the Wallraf-Richartz art museum outlined on the previous page. It is just a short walk to the Rathaus and Old Market.

A visit to the museum requires taking one of the guided tours to learn about the history of fragrance and enjoy interactive activities. Tours are available in English. Visits conclude with a stop in the museum store which, of course, focuses on cologne and fragrances. Tours may be booked in

Fragrance Museum
Photo Source: Raimond Spekking- Wikipedia

advance via the museum's website. Tours take roughly 45 minutes and several options are available.

Website: **www.Farina.org**

Address: Obenmarspforten 21, 50667 Köln

Subway: The closest subway stations are the Rathaus or Heumarkt stops. Both are a few minutes' walk east from here.

Fees: The 2023 adult rate for the guided tour is €8 and discounts are provided to holders of the Köln Card. There are additional fees for private tours and special tours such as the historical costume tour.

Hours: Normal hours: Open every day. Most days 10AM to 6PM, Sunday hours are 11AM to 6PM.

6-4711 Perfume Store & Museum / Dufthaus 4711:

The 4711 label of perfume began in the city of Cologne in 1799. While the company now has several perfumes, the original product the Echt Kölnisch Wasser, is still in production.

The first store for 4711 cologne is still open and tours are available in addition to an impressive store. The perfume itself, Eau de Cologne, or "Water from Cologne" was created in 1792 named by the inventor, Johann Maria Farina.

The 4711 Cologne Flagship Store
Photo Source: Raimond Spekking- Wikipedia

If you visit here, come primarily for the store. Tours and fragrance seminars are provided, but they are limited and must be booked in advance. Typically, the tours and seminars are limited to Saturdays.

Website: **www.4711.com**

Address: Glockengasse 4, 50667 Köln

Public Transportation: The bus has the closest stop at Offenbachplatz. Or take the subway to the Neumarkt stop and walk six minutes north and east from this station to reach the shop.

There is also a store, the **4711 Shop am Dom,** near the cathedral.

Fees: There is no fee to enter the store, except of course, the fees to purchase the perfumes. There is a small fee to take the historical guided tour or participate in one of the fragrance seminars.

Hours: Normal store hours: Monday to Saturday from 9:30AM to 6PM, slightly later on Saturday. Closed Sunday. Tour hours vary and the website should be checked for current available tours.

7-Roman Museum / Römisch-Germanisches Museum:

Some confusion may arise when looking into visiting this museum which focuses on the area's Roman history. One is a large facility near the cathedral. The smaller "Belgian House" (Belgisches Haus) sits a bit south and west from the cathedral area. As of this writing, the larger location near the cathedral is temporarily closed so activity and many exhibits have been moved to the Belgian House.

The goal of the museum is to display the archeological heritage of Cologne with exhibits that not only include the Roman settlements, but items dating back over 100,000 years to Paleolithic times and the hunter-gatherer periods.

Website: **www.Roemisch-Germanisches-Museum.de**

Belgian House location: Cäcilenstraße, 50667 Köln

Public Transportation: Take the subway to the Neumarkt station. From there, it is just a two block walk east to the museum.

Hours: Closed on Tuesday. Wednesday to Monday, the hours are 10AM to 6PM.

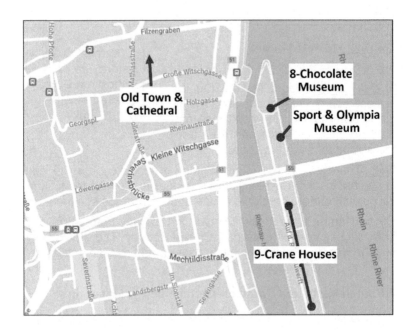

8-Cologne Chocolate Museum / Schokoladen Museum:

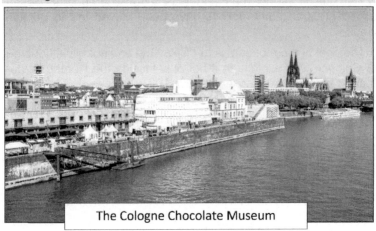

The Cologne Chocolate Museum

A museum dedicated to the history and making of chocolate, a fun destination for any age. Exhibits and tours cover the range of chocolate history dating back to the Mayans and Aztecs, up to current practices and production.

This is a relatively new museum and is celebrating its 30th anniversary in 2023. Since opening in 1993 it has become one of Germany's most popular museums.

The large facility sits on a narrow peninsula along the Rhine River. In addition to the two stories of exhibits inside, there is a large outdoor

Enjoy the museum's chocolate fountain.
Photo Source: N Angermann-Wikipedia

promenade with enjoyable views of the river and passing boat traffic. It also has excellent views of the cathedral and neighboring St. Martin Church.

The facilities inside include nearly 14,000 square feet (1300 sq meters) of exhibits, many of which are interactive. There is also a chocolate café and large shop.

Tours are available, but most are only provided in German. Check the website for current tour availability.

Website: **www.SchokoladenMuseum.de**

Address: Am Schokoladenmuseum 1a, 50678 Köln

Transportation: If you are coming from the cathedral area, consider doing this the fun way and catch the "Schoko-Express." This is a small tourist train which takes visitors from the cathedral area to the Chocolate factory. The website for this is **www.Bimmel-Bahnen.com.**

Other options include the Hop-On (City Tour) bus which stops here or catch the bus and take it to the museum. Unfortunately, the local subway system is not convenient to this museum.

Fees: Fees are fairly steep.[7] Many options are available varying by when you visit, group size, and age. If you have a Köln Card, you will be eligible for discounts. Cost to enter is slightly higher on weekends. Example adult fees: weekday €14,50 or weekend €16.

Hours: Open every day except some holidays. 10AM to 6PM.

9-Crane Houses / Kranhäuser:

Cologne's Crane Houses / Kranhäuser
Photo Source: Rolf Heinrich - Wikipedia

Immediately south of the Chocolate Museum and on the same narrow peninsula, is a set of three modern buildings, the Crane Houses, or Kranhäuser. These 17-story buildings were built in 2006 to be similar in shape to the harbor cranes which are used to load cargo onto ships and once had been active here.

---

[7] **Museum Fees:** All fees cited in this guide are as of mid-2023 and are subject to change.

Today, the three buildings are used for a mixture of residences and offices. For visitors to this area of Cologne, there is little else here in the way of attractions, shops, or restaurants. However, just strolling the riverfront at the base of these unique buildings provides some good photo opportunities.

Address: Brueckenstraβe 17, 50667 Köln

Transportation: There are several choices: The City Tour, Hop On, bus does take visitors to the nearby Chocolate Museu; take a city bus to the Schokoladenmuseum stop at the top of the peninsula which houses the crane houses and the Chocolate Museum; ride the tram to the Ubierring which sits slightly south of the crane houses.

10-Colonius Turm Köln:

It is reasonable for visitors to want to head to this TV tower and observation platform which stands tall over Cologne. Unfortunately, it has been **closed to visitors** since 1992.

The area where this tower sits is a good destination to explore the local park system. It sits near the center of a semi-circular green space which surrounds much of central Cologne.

A good alternative is to go to the observation deck at Cologne Triangle which is immediately across the Rhine from the center of town.

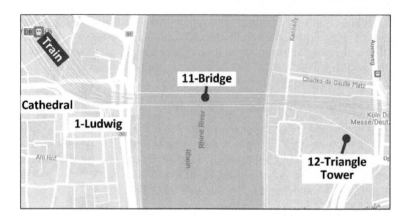

11-Hohenzollern Bridge / Hohenzollernbrücke:

Cologne's "Love Lock" bridge spans the Rhine and provides an enjoyable stroll from the cathedral area on the west to the eastern side or right bank. The right bank contains the Triangle Tower and a plaza with a statue of Kailer Wilhelm who had inaugurated the bridge.

When it was fully opened in 1911, the bridge provided travel for vehicles and trains. Today, it is primarily a train bridge, but one with an enjoyable pedestrian walkway lined with love locks.

The bridge, which is 1,342 feet long (409 meters), is Germany's busiest railway bridge.

During WWI,I the bridge miraculously survived the numerous bombing raids by the Allies. All other bridges nearby were destroyed. Unfortunately, the German's blew it up in 1945 in an effort to halt the advancing Allied troops. It was reopened in 1948.

The tradition of adding lovelocks to the bridge began in 2008 and today the number is estimated at 500,000 padlocks.

There is no fee to cross the bridge and coming here provides some excellent photo opportunities of Cologne's Cathedral and St. Martin Church.

12-Triangle Tower Cologne View / Köln Triangle:

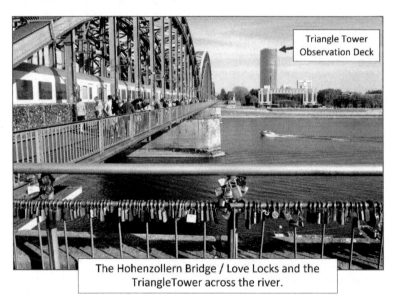

Triangle Tower
Observation Deck

The Hohenzollern Bridge / Love Locks and the TriangleTower across the river.

Across the Rhine from central Cologne is a tall office building, the Triangle Tower, which has an observation deck known as the Cologne View at the top. Ride the elevator to the 29th floor to an elevation of 341 feet (104 meters). Once here, there is a 360 viewing, open-air, platform of the city and suburbs.

77

Website: **www.KoelnTrianglePanorama.de**

Address: Ottopl 1, 50679 Köln

Getting Here: If you can walk and the weather is decent, consider walking across the Hohenzollern Bridge to reach the plaza and entrance to the tower.

The City Tour / Hop-On bus stops here or you can take the tram to the Deutzer Freiheit stop which is just one block south from the tower.

Fees: The adult fee as of mid-2023 to ride up to the top is €5. Children up to 12 are free. Advance ticket purchase is not needed.

Hours: Tower is closed during stormy weather. Normal hours are 11AM to 8PM Sunday to Thursday, and open until 10PM on Friday and Saturday.

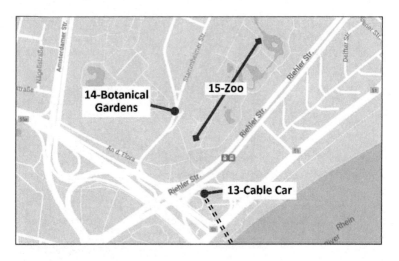

13-Cologne Cable Car / Kölner Seilbahn:

An interesting way to view Cologne from a lofty and moving viewpoint, is to take the cable car, or Kölner Seibahn (Also referred to as the Rhein Seilbahn), over the Rhine. There are two stations, one near the zoo on the left bank, and the other in a park area, the Rheinpark, on the right bank.

Your trip may start or end from either side. Each one-way trip is just six minutes in duration, and it spans over 3,000 feet (930 meters). Tickets may be purchased for a one-way or round-trip adventure.

The Cologne Cable Car / Kölner Seilbahn
Photo Source: Maxim 75 - Wikimedia Commons

Website: **www.Koelner-Seilbahnde.de**

Addreses:

- Left Bank (zoo area) station: Riehler Str. 180, 50735 Köln
- Right Bank (park area): Sachsenbergstraße 3, 51063 Köln

Fees: The adult fee as of mid-2023 for a one-way ticket is €5 and €7 for round trip. Fees for children 4-12 years are €3 and €4. Discounted combination tickets including the zoo and aquarium are also available. Fares are reduced for Köln Card holders.

Hours: Not open in the winter. Normal Spring-to-Fall hours are 10AM to 6PM.

~ ~ ~ ~ ~ ~

14- Flora Botanical Garden / Flora und Botanischer Garden:

Any number of superlatives could be used to describe this intricate and large botanical garden ranging from terms like spectacular to just plain beautiful. This sector of northern Cologne is an easy area to spend a full day when combined with the neighboring zoo and cable car.

Cologne's Flora Botanical Garden
Photo Source: Ladislaus Hoffner - Wikimedia Commons

This park, cologne's oldest, covers roughly twenty-eight acres (11.5 hectares) and displays more than 10,000 plant species. In addition to formal and informal gardens, visitors may tour several greenhouses and a Palm House which gives the feel of a tropical rain forest.

Website: **www.Freudeskries-Flora-Kroeln.de**

Address: Alter Stammerheimer Weg, 50735 Köln

Getting Here: Parking is near the entrance or take the tram to the Zoo/Flora station.

Hours: Open daily from 8AM to dusk.

15- Cologne Zoo / Koelner Zoo:

Cologne's zoo complex, which includes the three-story aquarium, is one of Germany's most popular zoos. It has a diverse collection with more than 10,000 animals. Among the popular attractions is an elephant park, adventure park, and large children's zoo.

The nearly fifty acres (20 hectares) include children's play areas, a theater, restaurant and shops. Look for the great ape jungle house. It is considered to be one of Europe's most immersive exhibits for the several specials living here.

Website: **www.KoelnerZoo.de**

Address: Riehler Strasse 173, 50735 Köln

Fees: A Day Pass which includes both the zoo and aquarium, as of mid-2023 are: Adults €23 and Children €11. Tickets may be purchased at the gate or in advance via the website.

Getting Here: The easiest way to travel to the zoo and neighboring botanical garden is to take the tram to the Zoo/Flora station. From there, it is a very short walk to the entrance.

Hours: Vary slightly by the season. March to October from 9AM to 6PM and November to February 9AM to 5PM.

~ ~ ~ ~ ~ ~

8: Shopping in Central Cologne

Finding new shopping and dining experiences when visiting a new city is part of the fun. Dining preferences can vary as greatly as your preferences for cuisine type or according to your budget.

The good news for visitors to central Cologne is that the areas where the best shopping, enjoyable beer gardens, and restaurant are often coincide. This chapter, for the most part, focuses on where in town to visit with a geographical constraint of central Cologne or Innenstadt. If you wish details on specific shops or restaurants, consider using one of the apps listed in the Preface.

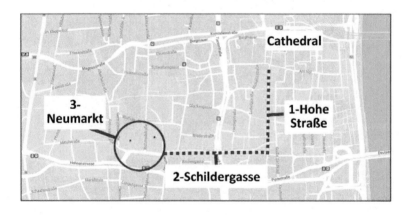

Three subsets of Innenstadt are listed here. Each of these are easy to reach from the cathedral area on foot or by a short tram/subway ride. The three areas combine to create one large shopping mecca which includes bustling shopping streets plus indoor malls.

1-Hohe Strasse / Hohe Straße: There are two very popular pedestrian-only shopping streets in Cologne and both rank among the best and busiest in all of Germany. The Hohe Strasse runs north-to-south for a bit over a quarter mile. It starts near the cathedral and goes until it intersects with the other popular shopping street, the Schildergasse.

This is a shopping heaven, but caution, it can be a very busy place, especially during holiday periods. This is an area not just for visitors and area specialties, but for local shopping as well. Come here for everything from clothing boutiques to popular chains such as Lego or H & M.

Cologne's Schildergasse shopping street.
Photo Source: Graphy Archy - Wikimedia Commons

2-Schildergasse: This east-west pedestrian shopping stretches for a third of a mile and connects Hohe Strasse with the Neumarkt park and shopping area. This, too, is an extremely popular and often crowded area with an estimated 15,000+ people per hour visiting here during peak shopping times. In addition to shopping, there are several restaurants along the main avenue and on the smaller connecting lanes.

One good way to reach the area is to take the subway to the Neumarkt station. This plaza, which has a park at the center, is adjacent to Schildergasse, the mall, and large stores in the Neumarket area.

3-Neumarkt & Neumarkt Passage: The Neumarket area, which sits at the western end of the Schildergasse shopping street, presents a different shopping experience. This is an area of shopping malls instead of pedestrian streets. There are two mid-size malls standing side-by-side and each has a mixture of department stores, boutique clothing, electronics, and restaurants.

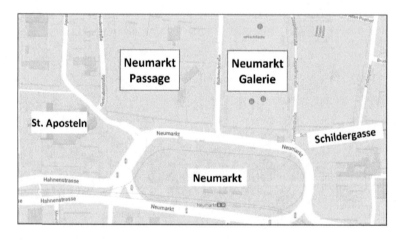

The two malls are:

- Neumarkt Passage: **www.NeumarktPassage.de**
- Neumarkt Galerie : **www.NeumarktGalerie.com**

9: Beer Halls & Kölsch Beer

Okay, this is Germany and enjoyment of beer in Cologne is every bit as ardent as in Munich and Bavaria. In Cologne, there is a special beer type which absolutely dominates the scene... **Kölsch Beer**. It is common in Germany for each area to have its own local beer and Kölsch beer is very much the pride of the region.

Cologne and Kölsch Bier - A fun combination.

To best enjoy the local beer and sample the most popular brews such as Früh, visit one or more of the beer halls, German restaurants, or gardens here. This chapter cites several of the more popular destinations, but this is far from being a complete list as many establishments serve local beer, often to the exclusion of beers from other areas.

Some German Beer Terminology:

- **Bier** = beer (wouldn't it be great if all terms translated so easily).

- **Biergarten** = a beer garden. In theory, this is limited to facilities which serve beer outside.

- **Brauhaus** = brewery. Many area beer houses use this term in their name and description.

- **Bierpalast or Bierhalle** = used to describe a large beer hall or pub.

- **Hofbrau** = a German restaurant, typically with a focus on beer. The seating and service are set out in cafeteria style with long picnic-table-like wooden tables.

- **Klein** = a small beer

- **Gross** = a large beer (if you have several you might, in fact, become gross).

Kölsch Beer & Culture: This is the only beer to have a protected geographical status in Germany and is tightly defined as to the ingredients, fermentation process, and geography. To be designated as Kölsch, the brewery must be within 30 miles (50 kilometers) of Cologne and the brewing must follow a specific set of area guidelines called the Reinheitsgebot. This is in addition to overall German laws regarding how beer is brewed.

This beer is normally served in a bottle and is light and clear with a crisp taste unlike many heavy lagers which can be found in Germany. A part of the Kölsch beer culture is to drink it from specially shaped glass. Servers will come around continually providing fresh glasses unless you indicate that you are done. There is generally no need to order more as the process is ongoing.

Some Good Places to enjoy Kölsch Beer: Given the German beer culture, it will come as little surprise to learn that local beer may be found in a nearly unlimited number of establishments ranging from beer halls, to German restaurants, and a few traditional beer gardens.

In the heart of Cologne, there are several popular destinations which not only serve Kölsch beer, but are great places to taste area and German cuisine as well. Following, are highlights for a set of beer halls and restaurants which provide a fun experience and are all within a short walk of the cathedral area.

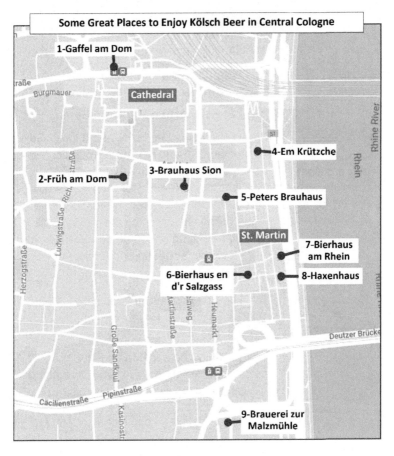

Some Great Places to Enjoy Kölsch Beer in Central Cologne

Suggested Beer Halls, Restaurants, & Gardens

The order listed here does not suggest any ranking or preference.

Map # & Establishment	Address & Details
-1- Gaffel am Dom	Bahnhofsvorpl 1, 50667 Köln **www.Gaffelamdom.de** Convenient to the train station and the cathedral. This is a beer hall and restaurant combination popular for live music. Set up in traditional Hofbrau style with a cozy atmosphere. Great for lunch or dinner. Come for the Gaffel label Kölsch beer.
-2- Früh am Dom	Am Hof 12-18, 50667 Köln **www.Frueh-Am-Dom.de** This is a combination, hotel with a large German restaurant, and beer garden/patio. Very close to the cathedral. It is a brewhouse/brauhaus for the Früh label. There are several different rooms to dine and imbibe here including a conservatory. This is a popular destination, so be prepared to wait for a bit for seating and service.
-3- Brauhaus Sion	Unter Taschenmacher 5-7, 50667 Köln **www.Brauhaus-Sion.de** More of a restaurant than traditional Brew Haus. Inviting, but slightly formal, atmosphere. Dining both inside and in their patio area. Try the Sion Kölsch label here along with a full array of German cuisine.

Suggested Beer Halls, Restaurants, & Gardens

The order listed here does not suggest any ranking or preference.

Map # & Establishment	Address & Details
	If you are looking for a fun venue for your wedding, check them out as they specialize in wedding receptions and events.
-4- Em Krützche	Am Frankenturm 1-3, 50667 Köln **www.Em-Kruetzche.de** Facing the Rhine River, with indoor and outdoor seating. A bit upscale, but highly rated and with a broad, German menu. Several differently styled rooms available. Noted dignitaries including US Presidents have dined here.
-5- Peters Brauhaus	Mühlengasse 1, 50667 Köln **www.Peters-Brauhaus.de** Located between the cathedral and St. Martin Church. A very popular restaurant specializing in area cuisine and, of course, Kölsch beer. More of a restaurant than a traditional beer house, but a great place to kick back and relax.
-6- Bierhaus en d'r Salzgass	Salgasse 5-7, 50667 Köln **www.Bierhaus-Salzgass.de** Tucked away in a small lane between St. Martin Church and the Hay Market, this beer house would be easy to miss. It is a lively, but fairly small, beer hall which specializes in the Päffgen label of Kölsch beer.
-7-	Franenwerft 27, 50667 Köln **www.Bierhaus-am-Rhine.de**

Suggested Beer Halls, Restaurants, & Gardens

The order listed here does not suggest any ranking or preference.

Map # & Establishment	Address & Details
Bierhaus am Rhein	Located along the riverfront with enjoyable views. Seating inside and outside in a relaxed environment
-8- Haxenhaus	Franenwerft 19, 50667 Köln **www.Haxenhaus.de** One of several brew houses lining the riverfront in this area. Haxenhaus has a traditional bierhaus arrangement and is another excellent spot to sit back, relax, and enjoy some Gaffel Kölsch. One of the larger establishments along this section of the river.
-9- Brauerei zur Malzmühle	Heumarkt 6, 50667 Köln **www.BrauereiZurMalzmeuhle.de** A family brewery which has been operating for over 160 years. Good location just south of the Hay Market area in the old town and close to the Chocolate Museum.

The above list highlights only some of the more popular beer halls and taverns in the heart of town. If you wish to explore out a bit further, such as going to the beer garden at Aachen Pond Beer Garden a bit west of central Cologne or one of the many small taverns in the Belgian Quarter, consider using one of the more popular apps such as the Cologne city Guide app to help find destinations which match your preferences

~ ~ ~ ~ ~ ~

10: Cologne Tours & Tour Providers

While many individuals prefer to manage visits to a new city and area on their own, there is a lot to say for joining a tour. The tour company can take you to locations and historic sights which might otherwise be overlooked or even closed to casual visitors.

In the case of visiting the Cologne and Bonn area, tours can range from full-day excursions to nearby towns to local walking tours. For museums and large churches, almost all provide tours. These tours will almost always enrich your visit and understanding of the area and its history.

This chapter provides an overview of the types of tours available and several of the leading companies. This is not a comprehensive list as the array of offerings is substantial, plus each of us has our own preferences of what sort of tour we would potentially find valuable.

Tour options in Cologne include :

- <u>Beer and Brewery Tours.</u> For many folks, there is little reason to keep on reading after seeing this.
- <u>Riverboat Tours</u> – a fun and relaxing way to see the city and many include lunch or dinner.
- <u>Walking Tours</u> – a great way to learn about the city and its history.

- <u>Bicycle Tours</u> – see the city and shoreline of the Rhine with a knowledgable guide.

> Most tour companies (see next page) provide several types of tours.

- <u>Hop-On Bus Tours</u> – a great way to see the city from a double-decker bus. See chapter 5 for more information.

- <u>Self-Guided Tours</u> – numerous options available and the Tourist Office is one of the best places to find many options.

- <u>Tours to Cologne from Other Cities</u>: If you want to visit here for a day from another city such as Amsterdam or Brussels, consider a private tour to Cologne.

- <u>Private Tours</u>: Tell the agency what you want to see and they can set up an itinerary designed for you.

An Excursion Tour Boat on the Rhine
Photo Source: Musement.com

Some Tour Agencies to Consider:

Many firms, local and worldwide, offer tours in and around Cologne, so you do not have to look far to find tours of interest. Also, the tours offered by the larger firms, such as Viator and Get Your Guide, tend to be the same or similar because these agencies tend to resell the same tours.

Visit Köln / Cologne Tourism Office: If you have not booked a tour in advance, the best service to start with is the local Tourist Office at **www.Cologne-Tourism.com.** There are many unique tours here and, should your plans change when you are in Cologne, it is generally easy to stop into the office near the cathedral to make adjustments and, in some cases, get a refund.

Tours offered include:

- Hop-On Bus and Tourist Train Tours – see chapter 5 for details.
- Walking Tours – several options. Caution, some are just in German.
- Boat Tours – including dinner excursions on the Rhine
- Beer Tours – Learn about Kölsch Beer the fun way.

Freewalk Cologne: As their name says, there are no upfront fees for these tours. Several options are available and most are group walking tours in central Cologne. Generous tipping is advised, to compensate for the lack of an initial charge.

Website: www.FreeWalkCologne.com

Tours offered include:

- Central Cologne Walking Tour – learn about the city's sights and way of life which would otherwise be easy to miss.

- Nighttime Cathedral Tour – learn about ghosts and murders and mayhem here.

- Belgian Quarter Tours -learn about the history of this popular district just on the western edge of town center.

- Beer Tour– Enjoy a Kölsch Brewery Tour – adults only.

~ ~ ~ ~ ~ ~

Tours by Locals: This firm operates worldwide and follows the model of focusing on private tours and using local guides. When researching their tours, you can view the profiles of the area guides in advance. Some tours can be customized to fit your preferences. A bit pricey, but the special attention provides for a great experience. Tours are typically half-day.

Website**: www.ToursByLocals.com** – then search for Cologne.

Tours offered include: Several unique tours available.

- Eue de Cologne – explore Cologne's Old Town and learn about the history of perfume here.

- Roman History Tour – Roman settlements are a big part of Cologne's past. Learn more about this history with a knowledgeable guide.

- Cathedral Tour - learn about its architecture and treasures with a private guide.

- Nazi Regime and History Tour– discover this dark chapter in Cologne's history. Visit the former Gestapo headquarters and other sites.

~ ~ ~ ~ ~ ~

Major Tour Resellers: Several notable and reputable firms compile an array of tours from a wide variety of tour providers, small and large. Available tours tend to be for groups, but some private tours are available. Tours will range from simple airport transfers to cathedral tours, walking tours, beer tours, and much more. The array of tours from these companies are very similar, so some price-comparison shopping can be beneficial. One good aspect of working with these firms is they all have customer-service lines to help you when problems arise.

Websites: (In each case, search for Cologne once you have gone to the firm's front/home page). These are some of the leading tour resellers, but many others such as Travelocity also provide these tours.

- Viator – a Trip Advisor subsidiary: **www.Viator.com**
- Get Your Guide - **www.GetYourGuide.com**
- Musement – **www.Musement.com**
- Visit A City – **www.VisitACity.com**

~ ~ ~ ~ ~ ~

11: Lodging in Cologne

A quick qualifier…it would take a guide far larger than this to detail all of the lodging options in and near central Cologne or Bonn, should you prefer to stay in this neighboring city. One helpful aspect of selecting lodging here is that Cologne is a city with a compact center, so the recommended geographical area is fairly small.

You can opt to select lodging out from the center a bit as the tram and subway system makes it easy to get into town. If your budget allows, strive to stay close to the cathedral area as great dining, sight-seeing, the train station, and most of the popular attractions are within an easy walk.

The array of lodging in central Cologne is staggering and well-rated options range from upscale hotels to apartment hotels. There are three subsets of central Cologne outlined here. They are near each other and each area will provide for easy access to the heart of Cologne.

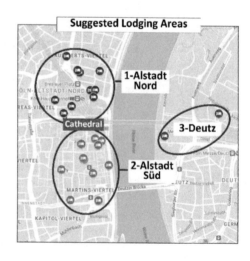

1. <u>Train Station Area / Altstadt-Nord</u>: Immediately next to, and slightly north of the Central Train Station.

2. <u>Old Town Area / Altstadt-Süd</u>: Numerous mid-size hotels and inns may be found close to, or just south of, the cathedral.

3. <u>Right Bank / Deutz area</u>: Lodging just across the river from central Cologne.

> The focus of this guide is on hotels and large inns, not Air B&B or similar lodging alternatives.

1 – Train Station Area / Alstadt-Nord:

In the area next to the main train station, Köln Hauptbahnhof, are many of Cologne's largest and most distinguished hotel properties. This location offers the advantage of proximity to trains and the local subway and tram systems. Walking distance into Old Town or to the river area is just a few blocks for most of the properties listed here.

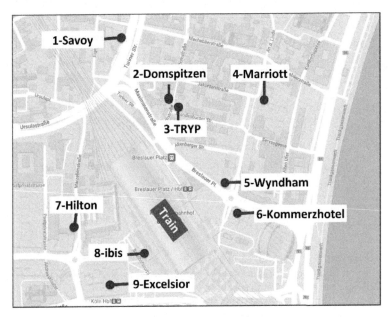

Several of Cologne's more prominent hotels, such as the Marriott
and Excelsior shown here, are near the train station.
Photo Source: Wikimedia Commons

Suggested Lodging in Alstadt Nord (Train Station Area)		
(All selected lodging has 3.5 or better rating)[8]		
Map # & Hotel	Address & Details	Rating
-1- Savoy Hotel	Turiner Str 9, 50668 Köln High-end luxury hotel and spa. www.Savoy.de	5 stars
-2- Hotel Domspitzen	Domstraße 23-25, 50668 Köln Modest, mid-size, boutique hotel. www.Hotel-Domspitzen.de	4 stars
-3- TRYP by Wyndham	Domstraße 10-16, 50668 Köln Mid-size, simple accommodations by Wynd- ham www.WyndhamHotels.com	3.5 stars

[8] **Hotel Ratings:** Ratings cited in this guide are a composite of author's
experience and other rating sources such as Trip Advisor, Google, and
Booking.com. No one single source was used.

Suggested Lodging in Alstadt Nord (Train Station Area)

(All selected lodging has 3.5 or better rating)[8]

Map # & Hotel	Address & Details	Rating
-4- Cologne Marriott	Johannisstraße 76-78, Köln Large, full-service, and modern. www.Marriott.com	4.5 stars
-5- Wyndham Koeln	Breslauer Pl. 2 2, 50668 Köln Mid-size hotel, small rooms. Business-class hotel. www.WyndhamHotels.com	4 stars
-6- Kommerzhotel Köln	Johannisstraße 30, 50668 Köln Next to train station. Contemporary, mid-size. www.KommerzHotel.eu	3.5 stars
-7- Hilton Cologne	Marzellenstraße 13, 50668 Köln Large, modern, full-service, & near train station. www.Hilton.com	4.5 stars
-8- Ibis Koeln Am Dom	Bahnhofsvorpl, 50667 Köln Budget hotel. Close to cathedral and train station. Small rooms and can be noisy. All.Accor.com	3.5 stars
-9- Excelsior Hotel Ernst	Trankgasse 1-5, 50667 Köln If you have a big budget, stay here. Luxury hotel with spa. Upscale throughout. www.ExcelsiorHotelErnst.com	5 stars

~ ~ ~ ~ ~ ~

2-Hotels in Old Town / Alstadt Süd Area:

The compact area just south of the cathedral, Cologne's Old Town, is an excellent area to stay if you wish to be in the center of the action for shopping, dining, and beer halls. At times, with many events occurring in the plazas, it can be noisy, but this tends to only be problematic if you want to open the windows of your hotel room.

Most lodging options here are smaller, boutique hotels, and a few apartment hotels. Several are along the river which can increase the enjoyment of your stay.

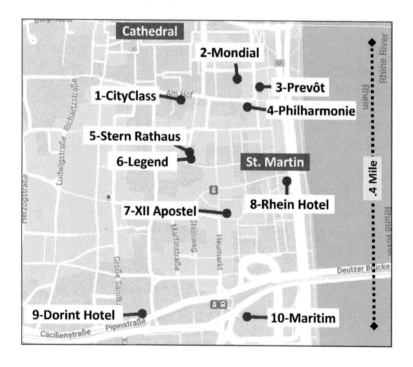

Suggested Lodging in Alstadt Süd (Old Town Area)

(All selected lodging has 3.5 or better rating)

Map # & Hotel	Address & Details	Rating
-1- CityClass Hotel Europa am Dom	Am Hof 34-46, 50667 Köln Close to cathedral and shopping. Full-service hotel with large rooms. www.CityClass.de	4 stars
-2- Hotel Mondial am Dom Cologne	Kurt-Hackenberg Platz 1, Köln Large hotel next to cathedral. Full-service. All.Accor.com	4 stars
-3- Prevôt Restaurant & Hotel	Auf dem Brand 4, 50667 Köln Boutique hotel with restaurant on the river. www.Prevot-Hotel.com	4 stars
-4- Hotel An der Philharmonie	Große Neugasse 36, 50667 Köln Contemporary boutique hotel tucked back on a quiet lane. www.Hadpc.com	3.5 stars
-5- Hotel Stern am Ratthaus	Bürgerstraße 6, 50667 Köln Small modern hotel close to the Old Market and many restaurants. www.Stern-Am-Rathaus.de	3.5 stars
-6- Legend Hotel	Bürgerstraße 2, 50667 Köln Boutique lodging with large rooms, in the heart of Old Town. www.LegendHotel.de	4 stars
-7- XII Apostel Hotel Albergo	Heumarkt 68-72, 50667 Köln Ornate boutique inn near the Hay Market. www.Xii-Apostel-Koeln.de	4 stars

Suggested Lodging in Alstadt Süd (Old Town Area)

(All selected lodging has 3.5 or better rating)

Map # & Hotel	Address & Details	Rating
-8- Rhein-Hotel St. Martin	Frankenwerft 31-33, 50667 Köln Small inn, facing the river and near St. Martin. www.RheinHotel-Koeln.de	4 stars
-9- Dorint Hotel am Heumarkt Köln	Pipenstraße 1, 50667 Köln Large, modern hotel near the Hay Market. Note, there is more than one Dorint in town. www.Hotel-Koeln-City.Dorint.com	4 stars
-10- Maritim Hotel Köln	Heumarkt 20, 50667 Köln Large hotel near the river, at the southern end of Old Town and close to Chocolate Museum. www.Maritim.de	4 stars

The large Maritim Hotel near Old Town and the Hay Market area.
Photo Source: Raimond Spekking - Wikimedia Commons

3-Hotels in Deutz / Right Bank Area:

If you are driving, the hotels on Cologne's right bank, or Deutz neighborhood, have the advantage of providing easy parking access. This area is away from the cathedral and old town which is a mixed blessing. On the downside, it does add an extra step of having to catch a tram or hike over the bridge to get into town. On the upside, there are great views across the river to central Cologne and this area tends to be less noisy, especially when major events are in progress. Another plus is the easy access to the lengthy promenade along the Rhine.

The Hyatt Regency Cologne.
Photo Source: Rolf Heinrich - Wikimedia Commons

Only three well-rated properties close to the river and the large tram station are cited here. Other large properties such as the Radisson Blu are not listed simply because they are not as central to town.

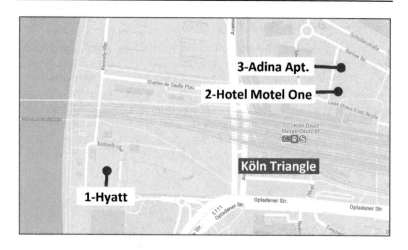

Suggested Lodging on the Right Bank

(All selected lodging has 3.5 or better rating)

Map # & Hotel	Address & Details	Rating
-1- Hyatt Regency Cologne	Kennedy-Ufer 2A, 50679 Köln Large hotel overlooking the river with great views of the city. www.Hyatt.com	4.5 stars
-2- Hotel Motel One Köln-Messe	Hans-Imhoff Str 3, 50679, Köln Large full-service hotel next to train and tram lines. www.Motel-One.com	4.5 stars
-3- Adina Apartment Hotel Cologne	Hans-Imhoff Str 1, 50679 Köln Big hotel with large rooms and kitchinettes. www.AdinaHotels.com	4.5 stars

~ ~ ~ ~ ~ ~

12: Bonn, Germany Overview

In chapter one, the word "vibrant" was used to summarize the city of Cologne. For Bonn, a larger set of terms is needed as this is a multi-faceted community. Good descriptors for this city of 330,000 could include terms such as: historic, cultural, active, and even quaint. Like Cologne, this is an easy city to explore on foot and, for the attractions which are a bit further out, there is an excellent transportation system available.

Bonn, Germany - a pleasant mix of old and new.

Bonn is just fifteen miles south of Cologne and is considered to be part of the same metropolitan area. Interconnectivity between the two cities via public transportation is excellent, making them easy to reach from one another for a day trip.

Although Bonn is easy to reach from Cologne, or even Dusseldorf for a one-day trip, a quick caution is in order... there is a lot to see here so you will have to pick-and-choose which sights to visit. The next chapter outlines the top points of interest here which range from popular squares to historic homes, and an incredible variety of museums.

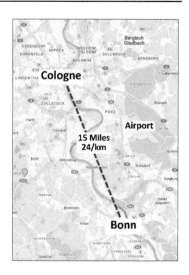

If you can spend two or more days here, you will be well rewarded. You will be able to view the treasures within Bonn as well as the sights close by such as Königswinter and Schloss Drachenburg. (See chapter 14)

The Altes Rathaus (Old Town Hall) on Marktplatz in central Bonn.

A Few Interesting Tidbits about Bonn:

- **Beethoven was born and lived here.** Ludwig van Beethoven was born in Bonn in 1770 and was one of seven children. He lived in Bonn until 1792 when he then moved to Vienna. Today, visitors may tour his birth home.

- **A Roman Settlement**: In the 1st century, Romans established the settlement of Castra Bonnensia here. Remnants of the ancient village were uncovered in 2006 and this is now an active archaeological site.

- **Bonn was briefly Germany's capital:** In 1949, Bonn became the capital of West Germany. It remained as the capital until 1990 when East and West Germany were unified, resulting in the capital moving to Berlin.

Beethoven statue in central Bonn.

- **Major corporations are here:** Several major companies have their headquarters here. Notables are the transport firm DHL and Deutsch Telekom which has the internet firm T-Mobile as one of their subsidiaries. For some added fun, the company which makes gummy bears, Haribo, is based here.

- **The U.N. has a base here**: We tend to associate the U.N. with either New York or Geneva, but this notable organization las a large campus in Bonn as well.

- **This is wine country**: Bonn sits at the base of a large German wine region, the Ahr Valley (Ahrtal). This area is known for its Pinot Noir grapes.

Layout of Bonn:

At the heart of Bonn and on the left bank of the Rhine, is a district called Bonn-Zentrum or Bonn Center. This fairly compact area is where most visitors will likely want to start their explorations. It is an area of pleasant plazas like the Market Square and impressive shopping lanes. This is also where major attractions such as the Beethoven Haus and the old town hall are. Bonn University and the Tourist Office are also here.

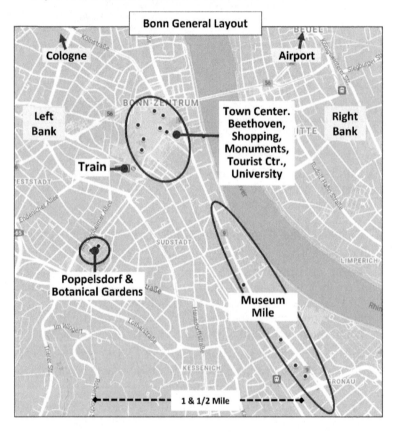

The main train station, the Bonn Hauptbahnhof, is on the edge of the old town and only a five-minute walk to Münsterplatz. It is a large plaza in the heart of town and the site of a monument to Beethoven.

One interesting aspect of Bonn's layout is the museum district, or the "Museum Mile." This area, which stretches south and east from the heart of town, holds a number of the city's most notable museums which are quite diverse in variety.

Chapter 13 provides information on the leading points of interest in and close to central Bonn.

A bit south of the old town and about a fifteen-minute walk from the train station, is the impressive botanical garden which has the huge and beautiful Poppelsdorf Schloss (palace) at its center. This distance is easily traveled by the area's transportation system.

Central Bonn has several large squares with restaurants and shops such as the Marktplatz.

Traveling to Bonn from Cologne:

When coming here from Cologne, and you are not driving, you have numerous options with the easiest being either the trains or tram systems. Trams have the advantage of having many points where you can get on and off, but the disadvantages of taking much longer and switching lines is often required. The author's recommendation is to utilize the local train system.

Trains generally take less than twenty minutes each way with numerous departures every day. Departing Cologne can be from the main train station near the cathedral (recommended) or from the Köln Sud (south) station. Advance purchase of tickets is not needed so simply go to the station, locate the next train, buy a ticket, and enjoy.

DB trains, **Deutsche Bahn**, connects Cologne to Bonn.

Arriving in Bonn brings you to the edge of Old Town and the shopping and business areas. There is access to area trams immediately out front of the station.

Website of App: Consider using the DB travel app or **Bahn.com** website to view routes and schedules and even ticketing.

Transportation in Bonn:

Trams & Buses: The transportation network in Bonn provides something of a good news/bad news scenario. This system is comprehensive with overlapping modes of travel which, for the good news, means you can get to almost anywhere in the city on trams, light rail, and buses. This also means it can be difficult for newcomers to learn, thus the bad news.

The Bonn Mobile App is a good tool to use for local transportation.

In addition to the complexity of the system itself, the array of ticket and travel pass offerings is daunting. So, a relatively simple solution is available…**download the Bonn Mobile app** and follow it closely. It also helps that detailed route maps can be found at every stop.

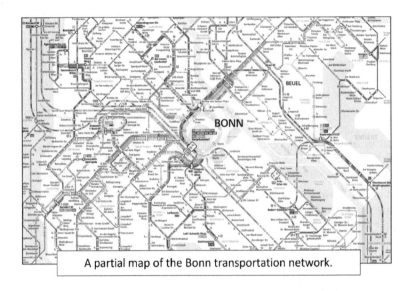

A partial map of the Bonn transportation network.

Most attractions in town are close to a tram stop with the one big exception of Schloss Drachenburg which sits off by itself on a hillside.

City Tour Bus / Hop-On: One enjoyable way to view the city and area is to take the Hop-On/Hop-Off bus in Bonn. Like many of these tour systems, this is a double-decker bus which enables you to get off at any of the 11 stops along the route. One notable caution is the tours only run a few times a day so if you do get off at one stop, it could be a long wait until the next one.

For full details, check **www.CityTour.de**

~ ~ ~ ~ ~ ~

13: Bonn Points of Interest
Museums-Shopping-Plazas

There are essentially four geographical areas where Bonn's most popular sites are located. With this in mind, the attractions in this chapter are organized by area rather than by type.

1 – Old Town or Bonn Altstadt. This area is less than a half-mile square. It is bordered on the west by the train station and on the east by the Rhine River. Head to this section of town to view the Beethoven house, Old Town, numerous squares, and shopping streets.

> **Discount Card**
>
> If you will be visiting several museums or using local transportation, consider acquiring the Bonn Regio Welcome Card. Go to **www.Bonn.de** for details.

2 – Museum Mile: An area stretching southeast from downtown, which includes five popular museums. For a bit of relaxation, consider heading over to the Friezeitpark, an expansive park, which roughly parallels the Museum Mile.

3 – Poppelsdorf Palace: One of the most photogenic areas of Bonn is the botanical garden and the Poppelsdorf Palace which is in its center. This attractive destination is about a half mile southwest from the train station and easy to reach by bus.

4 – Konigswinter: Although not a formal part of Bonn, this resort town and its castle, Schloss Drachenburg, are popular destinations for visitors to Bonn and included in many area tours. These sites are addressed in the following chapter.

1-Old Town / Bonn Altstadt Area:

Beethoven Haus. His birthplace and now a popular museum in Old Town Bonn.

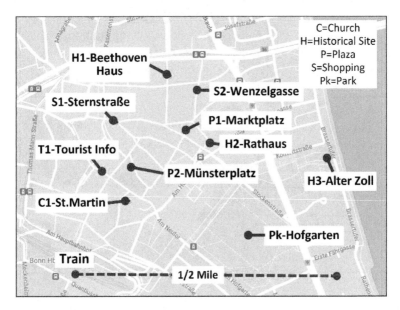

C=Church
H=Historical Site
P=Plaza
S=Shopping
Pk=Park

H1-Beethoven Haus

S2-Wenzelgasse

S1-Sternstraße

P1-Marktplatz

H2-Rathaus

T1-Tourist Info

P2-Münsterplatz

H3-Alter Zoll

C1-St.Martin

Pk-Hofgarten

Train

1/2 Mile

1 – Central Bonn Points of Interest		
Map Code	**Type**	**Name, Address & Description**
T1	Tourist Center	Tourist Information Center / Office De Tourisme • Stop in here for city passes, maps, and tour help. • Windeckstraße 1, 53111 Bonn • www.Bonn-Region.de
C1	Church	Minster of St. Martin's / Bonner Münster St. Martin • Roman Catholic church built in 11th to 13th centuries. • Am Hofgarten, 53111 Bonn
H1	Historical Sites	Beethoven-Haus Bonn • Beethoven's birthplace and museum. • Bongasse 22-24, 53111 Bonn • www.Beethoven.de
H2	Historical Sites	Bundesstadt Bonn – Altes Rathaus • Historic city hall bordering the Marktplatz. Built in Rococo style. • Markt 2, 53111
M3	Historical Sites	Stadtbefestingung Alter Zoll • 17th century fortress on the Rhine • Brassertufer, 53113, Bonn
P1	Plazas	Marktplatz • Large open square lined with shops and restaurants. A frequent site for markets and events.

1 – Central Bonn Points of Interest		
Map Code	**Type**	**Name, Address & Description**
P2		Münsterplatz • Large square adjacent to St. Martin church and department stores. • The Beethoven- Denkmal statue is here.
S1	Shopping Streets	Sternstraße • The longest and most popular pedestrian shopping street in Bonn. A great area to find boutiques and dining.
S2		Wenzelgasse • Popular shopping lane.
Pk	Park	Hofgarten Bonn • Open-park area adjacent to Bonn University.

Hofgarten Park - Adjacent to the University of Bonn.
Photo Source: Arabsalam - Wikimedia Commons

2-Museum Mile Area:

While many cities have their major museums scattered through-out town, in Bonn, a majority of them are in the same narrow stretch, giving the area the name of "Museum Mile." It is actually about two miles long. There are five notable museums here, four are close together with the fifth sitting a bit further south.

A website detailing the museums here along with guidance on current exhibits is: **www.MusemsMeileBonn.de.**

Every destination outlined here is easily reached by local trans-portation. Trams can take visitors to every attraction with the ex-ception of the Deutsches Museum, which is better reached via bus.

The Deutsches Museum - Science and Technology
Photo Source: Orcho - Wikimedia Commons

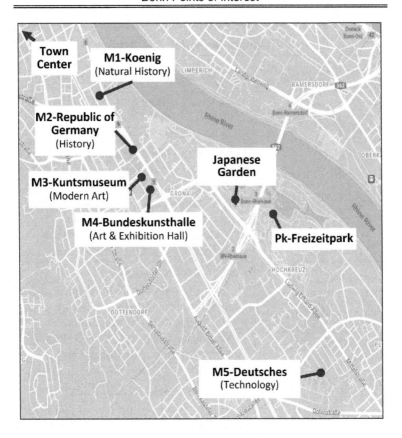

2 – Bonn's Museum Mile Area		
Map Code	Type	Name, Address & Description
M1	Natural History Museum	Museum Koenig • A museum dedicated to zoological studies and natural history. Focus is on the Blue Planet with large habitats which are great for kids to explore.

	2 – Bonn's Museum Mile Area	
Map Code	**Type**	**Name, Address & Description**
		• Museum Alexander Koenig, 53113 Bonn • Website: Bonn.Leibniz-lib.de/en
M2	History Museum	House of the History of the Federal Republic of Germany • German history since 1945 to current time. One of Germany's most popular museums. • Willy-Brant-Allee 14, 53113 Bonn • Website: www.Hdg.de
M3	Modern Art Museum	Kunst Museum Bonn • Art museum with a focus on modern and expressionism including post war German art.ar museums. • Willy-Brant-Allee 14, 53113 Bonn • Website: www.KunstMuseum-Bonn.de
M4	Exhibition Hall	Bundeskunsthalle / Federal Art Hall • This is cited by the city of Bonn as one of the museums on Museum Mile, but it is a large exhibition hall with a frequent focus on art and cultural events. • Friedrich-Ebert-Allee 4, 53113 Bonn • Website: www.Bundeskunsthalle.de
M5	Science & Technology Museum	Deutsches Museum Bonn • Expansive museum sitting a bit off by itself. Focus is on technology and artificial intelligence. Numerous interactive exhibits. • Ahrstraße 45, 53175 Bonn

2 – Bonn's Museum Mile Area		
Map Code	**Type**	**Name, Address & Description**
		• Website: www.Deutsches-Museum.de
Pk	Large, Multi-faceted Park	Freizeitpark Rheinaue Bonn • A large park of 395 acres (160 ha) which runs between the Rhine River and the Museum Mile. • This park encompasses numerous features such as a Japanese garden, lakes, trails, statue garden, restaurant, miniature golf, and more. • Ludwig=Erhard-Allee 20, 53175 Bonn

Freizeitpark Rheinaue

3- Poppelsdorf Palace & Botanical Gardens Area:

A modest walk of 10 to 15 minutes south of the train station is the attractive Poppelsdorf Palace (Schloss Poppelsdorfer). It includes surrounding gardens and the formal Botanical Gardens. Reachable by the local bus service. Nearby are two museums to add to the excursion.

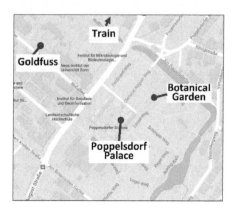

Poppelsdorf Palace (Schloss Poppelsdorfer): This 18th century Baroque palace is reminiscent of the times when Bonn was the political center of Germany. Today, the building is an administrative center for the University of Bonn, so it is not open to tours or casual visitors.

Poppelsdorf Palace & Botanical Gardens

Botanical Gardens/Schlossgarten: Visiting the gardens allows you to tour the grounds surrounding the palace and glasshouses which focus on different ecosystems such as the Rain Forest House. This set of gardens is operated by the university.

There is a fee to enter the grounds and hours vary by the season. The best time to come is from early April to the end of September. Normal hours are 10AM to 6PM during the Spring and Summer.

Address:Meckenheimer Allee 171, 53115 Bonn

Website: Bogart.Uni-Bonn.de

Goldfuss Museum / Goldfuß Museum: One block northwest from Poppelsdorf is a museum dedicated to paleontology which is managed by the University of Bonn. It has an extensive collection of fossils and dinosaur skeletons. Tours are available.

Hours: Normal hours are 9AM to 4PM, closed on Saturday.

Address: Naussallee 8, 53115 Bonn.

Website: www.ifgeo.uni-bonn.de

~ ~ ~ ~ ~ ~

14: Königswinter and Schloss Drachenburg

The quaint town of Königswinter is less than six miles south of central Bonn and is often thought of as one of its suburbs. Still, once you are here, it feels worlds away from any city due to the tall hills and natural setting.

This is an excellent day trip destination from either Bonn or Cologne. Both are easy to reach by train from Cologne or tram from

The Drachenfels Cog Railway in front of Schloss Drachenburg

Bonn. The one caveat to this statement is the enjoyment of this town, its castles, and the area is dependent on good weather. Given that most of the sites compel you to be outside, coming here on a rainy day is not advisable.

The most noted attraction here is the castle **Schloss Drachenburg** which sits on a promenade above the town. This castle is not all that there is to see here and Königswinter is often a stop for river cruises and for good reason. The town itself is attractive and streets near the river are lined with shops and restaurants. There is a long promenade along the river. In the hills above the town, there are two castles to visit plus a large natural area with hiking trails. If this was not enough, this is also wine country.

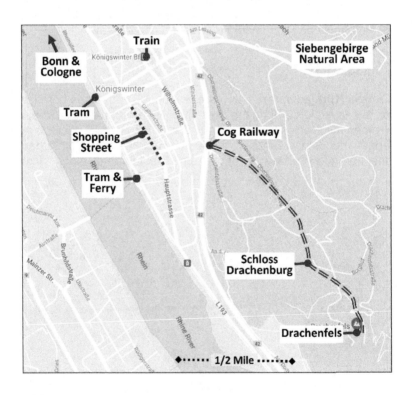

Traveling to here by Train or Tram:

- **From Bonn by tram:** Catch line 66 from Bonn's train station and stay on until you get to the Königswinter stop. From there, it is less than a five-minute walk into the heart of town or an eight-minute walk to the cog rail station, which takes riders up to the castles. Trains, for most individuals, do not work as well from Bonn because a change in route is needed. Taking the tram is direct.

- **From Cologne by train:** This train trip from Cologne's main train station to the Königswinter station only takes around 40 to 50 minutes each way and trains run frequently. Get off at Königswinter BF train station which sits slightly uphill from the town and the river. From here, it is about a seven-minute walk into town or a ten-minute walk to the cog railway.

Köningswinter Area Highlights:

Central Königswinter: There are two popular stretches here for visitors to explore. Along the river, there is the scenic walk "Rhein Promenade Königswinter" and, in the heart of town, there is a lengthy pedestrian shopping street, the Hauptstrasse. Both areas offer a good array of shops and restaurants along with

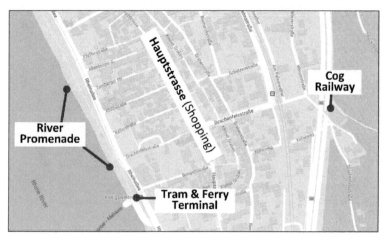

sightseeing. Everything in town is within a few minutes' walk plus a short distance to trams, trains, and ferries.

Cog Railway / Drachenfelsbahn: Germany's oldest cog railway provides a fun way to work your way up the hills from Königswinter to the two most popular area destinations of Drachenburg Castle at the midpoint and the peak of the mountain at Drachenfels. The total distance is about a mile (1.5km) and takes visitors to 948 feet elevation. (290 meters).

The Drachenfels Cog Railway
Photo Source: Slick - Wikipedia

Frequency: Trains run every 30 minutes, with some reduction in frequency in January and February.

Tickets: May be purchased online at the ticket office. Tickets are available either as round-trip or your selection of just the ascent or descent. For round trip adult fare, expect to pay around €12, with fares subject to change.

Website: **www.Drachenfelsbahn.de**

Drachenburg Castle / Schloss Drachenburg: This is a fairly modern palace, as it was built in 1884, but done so to give a mix of styles from earlier periods including Gothic and Renaissance. It was initially built as a private villa, but crafted to give the feeling of a castle or palace. After WWII, it was largely abandoned until 1963 when it was then fully restored.

Today, this is a popular visitor attraction which includes guided tours. Tours are required to visit the inside. A variety of tours are available, with the standard 45-minute group tour being the most popular. Private tours are also available. Check the website for details on the various tours. If you are coming during the summer months, advance purchase is advised.

There are two main ways to reach the castle from the town of Königswinter below. If you have come to town via boat, train, or tram, consider taking the cog railway. Another enjoyable way to reach the castle is on foot. The walk is roughly one kilometer (varies by your starting point) from the town's large parking lot. The walk is enjoyable, but a bit uphill.

Hours: This varies by the season but, during high season, it is open from 11AM to 6PM.

Cost: Tickets are available for adults, children, and families. A single adult ticket as of mid-2023 is €8 and a family ticket for 4 is €18.

Website: **www.Schloss-Drachenburg.de**

Schloss (Castle) Drachenburg. Overlooking Köningswinter and Bonn in the distance.

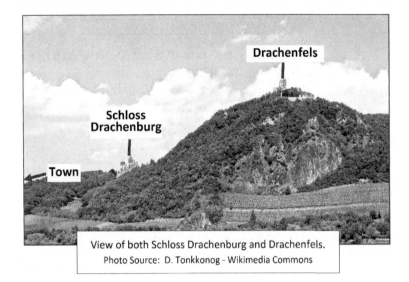

View of both Schloss Drachenburg and Drachenfels.
Photo Source: D. Tonkkonog - Wikimedia Commons

Drachenfels: It is easy to get confused when visiting here as two of the leading destinations have similar names, Schloss Drachenburg, a castle, and the other location, Drachenfels which is a mountaintop castle ruins and overlook.

This site, which sits high above Schloss Drachenburg, is best reached by the Cog Railway. You can also consider taking that fun train up and then walking down.

At the top, this site, which is formally known as Drachenfels Siebengerbirge, is primarily an overlook which sits at 1,053 feet. There are the ruins of a 12th century castle here in addition to a restaurant and conference center called Der Drachenfels.

There is no fee to visit the grounds and enjoy the views of the Rhine River below you.

Website: **www.Drachenfels.net**

~ ~ ~ ~ ~ ~

Appendix: Websites for Additional Information

To help you expand your knowledge of this area, several online reference sites are listed here. Cologne and Bonn have a wealth of online references and tourism sites which can help in planning your trip.

The following is a list of online references for this city and the area. The purpose of this list is to enhance your understanding before embarking on your trip. Any online search will result in the websites outlined here plus many others. These are listed as they are professionally done and do not only try to sell you tours.

1-Cologne & Bonn Area Websites.	
Website Name/Type	**Website address and description**
Cologne Tourism	**www.Cologne-Tourism.com** Details on the city of Cologne, hotels, activities, tours, and restaurants. Another site crafted for visitors to Cologne is: **www.Cologne.de**
Bonn Tourism	**www.Bonn.de** Tourist office website for Bonn and area, including helps on tours, sights, dining.

1-Cologne & Bonn Area Websites.

Website Name/Type	Website address and description
Events Calendar	**www.AllEvents.In/Cologne** Details on all upcoming events and conferences in the city of Cologne, and other cities.
City Discount Cards	Bonn and Cologne each have discount programs for visitors on their tourist office sites. - **www.Cologne-Tourism.com** - **www.Bonn-Region.de.** **www.Bonn.de**
Cologne City Tour /Hop-On Bus	**www.CityTour.de** Routes and schedules for Cologne's Hop-On bus tour program and ability to purchase tickets.
Hop-On Trolley in Cologne	**www.BimmelBahnen.com** A small tourist train in Cologne. Details on the routes and tours available.
Cologne Cathedral	**www.Koelner-dom.de** History of the cathedral and details on the many treasures it holds. For info on tours and south-tower visits go to: **www.DomFuehrugen-Koelnn.de**
Trip Advisor	**www.TripAdvisor.com** – then search for Cologne, Bonn, or other towns of interest. One of the best overall travel sights with details and reviews on most attractions, restaurants, and hotels.

1-Cologne & Bonn Area Websites.	
Website Name/Type	**Website address and description**
Bonn Museum Mile	**www.Museums.MeileBonn.de** Details and a map on the five museums in Bonn which make up the Museum Mile.

2-Transportation Information and Tickets	
Website Name/Type	**Website Address & Description**
Cologne Transporta-tion	**www.Kvb.com or www.Kvb.Koeln** Details on city and area trams, subways, and buses including ability to purchase passes.
Cologne-Bonn Airport	**www.Cologne-Bonn-Airport.com** Helpful info on the layout of the airport, and transportation options.
Airport Trans-portation	Two recommended services for ground trans-portation to and from Cologne-Bonn airport. - **www.Sixt.com** - **www.WelcomePickups.com**
Rome 2 Rio	**www.Rome2Rio.com** An excellent site for comparing travel times and costs across different modes of transpor-tation. Tickets may be booked from this site.
Cologne Bi-cycle Rental	**www.Kvb-Rad.de** Details on the bike share service and provi-sions to set up an account which will enable you to rent bicycles in Cologne.
Train Ticket Resellers	Several services enable you to purchase train tickets online prior to your trip, including:

2-Transportation Information and Tickets	
Website Name/Type	**Website Address & Description**
	- RailEurope.com - TrainLine.com - Eurorailways.com These sites are a good place to check schedules and train availability for all train companies servicing most areas in Europe.

3-Tour and Hotel Booking Sites	
Service	Website address and description
Hotel Sites	Numerous online sites enable you to review and book hotels online. Most of these sites also resell tours. - Booking.com - Hotels.com - Expedia.com - Travelocity.com
Tour Resellers	Many companies, such as the ones listed here, provide a full variety of tours to the Cologne and Bonn area. The offerings are similar, but the research is helpful as some firms offer unique services and tours. - GetYourGuide.com - ToursByLocals.com - Viator.com - Musement.com - WorldTravelGuide.net

~ ~ ~ ~ ~ ~

Index of Sights in this Guide

Starting-Point Guides

This guidebook on Cologne & Bonn is one of several *Starting-Point Guides*. Each book in the series is developed with the concept of using one enjoyable city as your basecamp and then exploring from there.

Current guidebooks are for:

- **Bordeaux, France** and the Gironde Region
- **Dijon, France** and the Burgundy Region.
- **Geneva, Switzerland** and the Lake Geneva area.
- **Gothenburg, Sweden** and the central coast of western Sweden.
- **Lille, France** and the Nord-Pas-de-Calais Area
- **Lucerne, Switzerland,** and the Lake Lucerne region.
- **Lyon, France** and the Saône and Rhône confluence area.
- **Nantes, France** and the western Loire Valley
- **Reims & Épernay,** France the heart of the Champagne region
- **Salzburg Austria** and central Austria
- **Strasbourg, France** and the central Alsace area.
- **Stuttgart, Germany** and the Baden-Wurttemberg area.
- **Toledo, Spain** and the Don Quixote route.
- **Toulouse, France,** and the Haute-Garonne region.

Updates on these and other titles may be found on the author's Facebook page at:

www.Facebook.com/BGPreston.author

Feel free to use this Facebook page to provide feedback and suggestions to the author or email to: cincy3@gmail.com

Printed in Great Britain
by Amazon